THEMES
for early years

SPRING

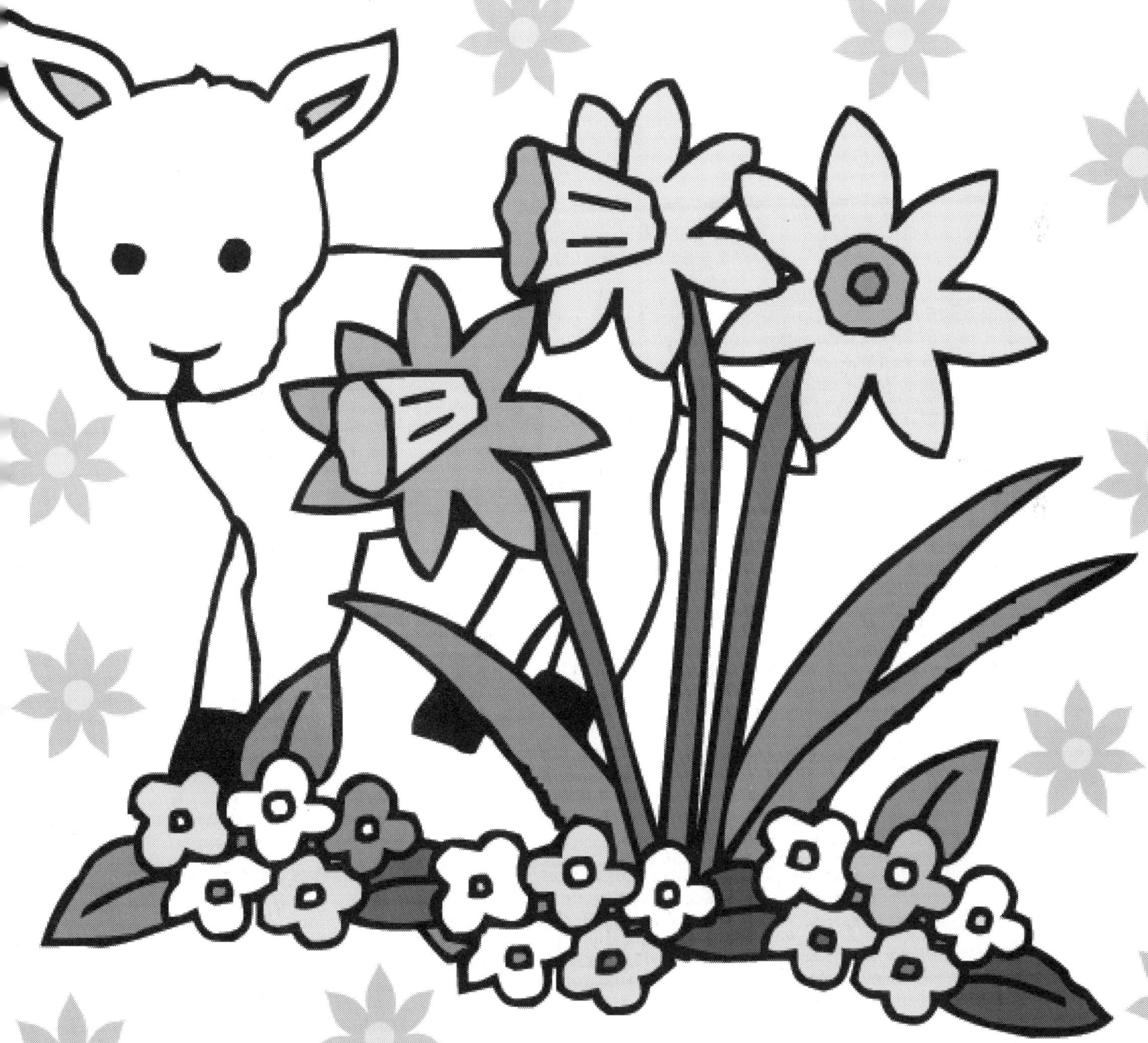

ANNE FARR & JANET MORRIS

Authors Anne Farr and Janet Morris
Editor Jane Bishop
Series designer Lynne Joesbury
Designer Glynis Edwards
Illustrations Chris Russell
Cover Lynne Joesbury
Action Rhymes, Poems and Stories compiled by Jackie Andrews
Songs compiled by Peter Morrell

Designed using QuarkXpress
Processed by Scholastic Ltd, Leamington Spa

Published by Scholastic Ltd, Villiers House, Clarendon Avenue, Leamington Spa, Warwickshire CV32 5PR

© 1998 Scholastic Ltd Text © 1998
1 2 3 4 5 6 7 8 9 8 9 0 1 2 3 4 5 6 7

The publishers gratefully acknowledge permission to reproduce the following copyright material:
Jackie Andrews for 'Wake Up - it's Spring' © 1998, Jackie Andrews, previously unpublished; **Clive Barnwell** for 'Spring! Spring! Spring!' © 1998, Clive Barnwell, previously unpublished; **Ann Bryant** for 'New Life' © 1998 Ann Bryant, previously unpublished; **Susan Eames** for 'Spring Cleaning' and 'I'm a Frog' © 1998, Susan Eames, previously unpublished; **Anne Farr** for the retelling of ***The Selfish Giant*** by Oscar Wilde © 1998, Anne Farr, previously unpublished; **Anne Farr and Janet Morris** for the retelling of ***The Story of Persephone*** © 1998, Anne Farr and Janet Morris, previously unpublished; **Jean Gilbert** for 'Spring Cleaning' © 1998, Jean Gilbert, previously unpublished; **Trevor Harvey** for 'The New Spring Hat' and 'Winter To Spring' © 1998, Trevor Harvey, previously unpublished; **Hazel Hobbs** for 'Pancakes' and 'Spring Salmon' © 1998, Hazel Hobbs, previously unpublished; **Penny Kent** for 'Holi' © 1998, Penny Kent, previously unpublished; **Karen King** for 'Daisy's Spring Clean' © 1998, Karen King, previously unpublished; **Johanne Levy** for 'Spring Blossom' © 1998, Johanne Levy, previously unpublished; **Wes Magee** for 'I Like The Park', 'Mad March Hare' and 'Valentine's Day Card' © 1998, Wes Magee, previously unpublished; **Tony Mitton** for 'The Gosling Song' and 'Seed Needs' © 1998, Tony Mitton, previously unpublished; **Janet Morris** for 'Here Comes The Rain' © 1998, Janet Morris, previously unpublished; **Judith Nicholls** for 'Weatherwise' © 1998, Judith Nicholls, previously unpublished; **Sue Nicholls** for 'Daffodil' © 1998, Sue Nicholls, previously unpublished; **Sue Palmer** for 'Boing! Boing! Boing!' © 1998, Sue Palmer, previously unpublished; **Jan Pollard** for 'Wake Up' © 1998, Jan Pollard, previously unpublished; **Coral Rumble** for 'It Must Be Springtime', 'Trumpet of Spring', 'Butterfly Inside' and April Fool's Day' © 1998, Coral Rumble, previously unpublished; **Catherine Wheaton** for 'Maypole' and 'It's Bank Holiday Monday!' © 1998, Catherine Wheaton, previously unpublished; **Stevie Ann Wilde** for 'The New Nest' © 1998, Stevie Ann Wilde, previously unpublished; **Margaret Willetts** for 'Visiting The Farm' © 1998, Margaret Willetts, previously unpublished.
British Library Cataloguing-in-Publication Data A catalogue record for this book is available from the British Library.

ISBN 0-590-53807-1

The right of Anne Farr and Janet Morris to be identified as the Authors of this work has been asserted by them in accordance with the Copyright, Designs and Patents Act 1988.

All rights reserved. This book is sold subject to the condition that it shall not, by way of trade or otherwise, be lent, hired out or otherwise circulated without the publisher's prior consent in any form of binding or cover other than that in which it is published and without a similar condition, including this condition, being imposed upon the subsequent purchaser.

No part of this publication may be reproduced, stored in a retrieval system, or transmitted, in any form or by any means, electronic, mechanical, photocopying, recording or otherwise, without the prior permission of the publisher. This book remains copyright, although permission is granted to copy pages where indicated, for classroom distribution and use only in the school which has purchased the book, or by the teacher who has purchased this book and in accordance with the CLA licensing agreement. Photocopying permission is given for purchasers only and not for borrowers of books from any lending service.

CONTENTS

INTRODUCTION

This book aims to provide a 'treasure chest' of lively, practical and workable activities which are suitable for use by adults working with children of varying abilities and levels of maturity in the three to six year age range. All the activities, while firmly rooted in structured play, are designed to prepare children for the National Curriculum and Scottish 5–14 National Guidelines. The activities also fit well into the six Areas of Learning for under-fives, recommended by the School Curriculum and Assessment Authority in the document Nursery Education: Desirable Outcomes for Children's Learning on entering Compulsory Education.

Each activity has a specific National Curriculum subject focus but clearly learning in the early years is a 'seamless robe', and opportunities to help children develop all the skills, knowledge, concepts and attitudes that are an essential ingredient in early years education have been included.

USING THEMES

There are numerous ways of approaching a topic on 'Spring' and there are many opportunities to explore sub-themes. Chapters in this book cover the themes of:

1. Spring weather
2. Outdoor signs of spring
3. Spring traditions
4. Spring around the world
5. Animals in spring
6. New beginnings

Many of the activities allow children to work from firsthand experiences and also enable them to build on their previous knowledge and understanding. Opportunities are provided for children to discuss and explore familiar situations and develop their own knowledge and understanding of the many events and wonders associated with the season of spring.

CROSS-CURRICULAR LINKS

Many people working with young children choose to teach through cross-curricular themes because of the advantages presented by using an integrated approach. This method offers the opportunity for children to develop a broad range of concepts, skills and attitudes in all areas of the curriculum within an appropriate developmental context. For example, the children's communication skills can be developed through discussion, writing, drawing, role play, singing and modelling. Mathematical and scientific concepts can be explored as children engage in practical activities, for example cooking, movement and building. Observational and manipulative skills should be encouraged as children create and interact with displays and investigate artefacts and materials. Personal and social skills will be enhanced as children work individually, collaboratively in pairs, or within small groups, and as they investigate the importance of spring in people's lives.

HOW TO USE THIS BOOK

'Spring' is one of a series of books written specifically for adults working with young children at home, in playgroups, nurseries, nursery classes or schools.

Within each chapter, the first activity encapsulates and introduces the other activities in the chapter so that you can undertake the initial activity alone or select from the supporting activities as appropriate. The book contains material either for a long-term project or for a few activities linked to other books and themes.

The content of the book has been organised to allow versatility of use, providing a complete topic pack or an additional resource to supplement your own ideas.

However you choose to use the material, you can adjust the activities and resources to suit the particular needs of the young children in your care.

TOPIC WEB

The topic web on pages 8–9 is designed to aid long and short-term planning by showing how each activity relates to the National Curriculum and Scottish 5–14 Guidelines. To ensure that the children receive a broad and balanced curriculum, the topic web has been designed with an even distribution of activities between subjects. Although each activity has been given a main subject focus, most will also make important contributions to other subject areas, for example an activity identified as having a mainly historical basis will often include speaking and listening and so develop language skills.

ACTIVITY PAGES

Each chapter in this section focuses on a particular theme of 'Spring', and each individual activity is linked to a subject in the early years curriculum. For each activity a learning objective is identified which shows the main subject area and explains the purpose of the activity.

A suggestion is given for the appropriate group size, but individual circumstances may influence your choice of the number of children in the group. For example, having adult helpers may mean more children are able

to participate in an activity than is suggested. Under 'What you need', a list of materials and equipment needed before the activity can begin is provided and any preparatory work necessary, such as organising equipment or making labels, is listed. If the children need to have any previous experience or knowledge which is essential to the success of the activity this is also provided.

Step-by-step instructions are outlined on how to introduce each activity and guidance is offered on what the children should do. Although explicit instructions are given, a certain amount of flexibility is required, and most of the activities can be adapted for different levels of ability.

The main discussion points are identified, though it is important to adopt a flexible approach and allow the children to lead the conversation into other, equally valid areas. Sometimes activities involve adult intervention throughout, while others may lend themselves to an introductory session to stimulate the activity or as a summary discussion after the activity has been carried out. Whenever possible, encourage the children to share their ideas with a friend, an older child or adult helper as well as yourself.

Follow-up ideas for extending each activity, both within the subject and its associated areas, are also listed. Be prepared to follow up ideas which the children suggest, even if it develops the topic in a slightly different way to the one you had originally planned. It is important to allow the children the opportunity to experience self-directed tasks in this early stage of their education.

DISPLAY

Ideas for how to set up stimulus displays linked to the various themes of 'Spring' are provided in this chapter. A list of the materials required, instructions on how to assemble the displays and points for discussion are included. Most of the displays are interactive and whenever possible you can encourage the children to help collect and select resources and to assemble the display. Always allocate plenty of time for children to examine the displays individually and organise a group or class discussion time to talk about them.

ASSEMBLIES

This chapter provides ideas for planning assemblies or group sharing times related to the theme. Each assembly has its own practical ideas on how the children can be encouraged to contribute, to reflect on the specific theme, and a relevant prayer and song are suggested.

RESOURCES

A useful selection of stories, poems, action rhymes and songs linked with the 'Spring' topic are given. Much of the material is new and has been specially commissioned to complement the topic. All of these resources are photocopiable.

PHOTOCOPIABLE SHEETS

Eight photocopiable pages, each linked with a specific activity detailed earlier in the book, are provided. Before you hand out the sheets, make sure that the children understand how to carry out the activity, and that any new vocabulary is fully explained. Allow time to discuss the completed sheet with each child in order to assess how much they have understood.

RECOMMENDED MATERIALS

Details of story books, information books, poetry, music and songs linked to the topic are listed on the final page. In addition, encourage the children to bring their own favourite stories, poems and songs which focus on 'Spring' to share with the group.

EXPRESSIVE ARTS

ART

MUSIC

PE/DRAMA

ENGLISH

RE/RELIGIOUS AND MORAL EDUCATION

Planning towards the National Curriculum and the Scottish National guidelines 5–14

MATHEMATICS

ENVIRONMENTAL STUDIES

DESIGN AND TECHNOLOGY

SCIENCE

HISTORY / PEOPLE IN THE PAST

GEOGRAPHY / PEOPLE AND PLACE

PHOTOCOPIABLE

PREPARING FOR PRIMARY SCHOOL

THE NATIONAL CURRICULUM

The National Curriculum was established to standardise the subjects and subject content taught to every child in the country at all levels of education. The intention is that all schools teach the same subjects for the same amount of time each week, so that any child moving to another part of the country is not at a disadvantage. The National Curriculum subjects are: English, Mathematics, Science, History, Geography, Design and Technology, Information Technology, RE, Art, Music and PE.

The National Curriculum programmes of study apply to children who have reached their fifth birthday. Prior to this, an early years curriculum which is founded on the principles of active learning, first hand experiences and physical and sensory play, with plenty of time, space and sensitive adult support, will go a long way towards establishing a firm foundation for future learning of the National Curriculum.

THE DESIRABLE OUTCOMES

Before compulsory school, children are working towards Level One of the National Curriculum. The SCAA publication ***Nursery Education: Desirable Outcomes for Children's Learning on Entering Compulsory Education*** provides guidance for the education of the under-fives across six Areas of Learning. They are: Personal and Social Development, Language and Literacy, Mathematics, Knowledge and Understanding of the World, Physical Development and Creative Development. The activities in this book, while preparing the children for the National Curriculum, also link closely to these Areas of Learning, following a play-based rationale for learning. Similar guidelines exist for Wales, Scotland and Northern Ireland and the ideas in this book can be applied equally well to the guidance documents published for these countries.

THE SCOTTISH NATIONAL GUIDELINES 5–14

In Scotland, there are National Guidelines for schools on what should be taught to children between the ages of five and fourteen.

These National Guidelines are divided into six main curriculum areas: English Language, Mathematics, Environmental Studies, Expressive Arts, Religious and Moral Education, and Personal and Social Development.

Within these main areas, further subjects are found, for example, 'Expressive Arts' includes art and design, drama, music and PE. Strands are also identified within each subject, for example Mathematics includes problem solving and enquiry, and shape, position and movement.

CHAPTER 1
SPRING WEATHER

Help children develop their understanding of time by introducing the idea of spring weather bringing changes which the children can see around them. Learning about lighter days and warmer weather brings opportunities for children to match seasonal activities, create a display of spring clothing and learn some weather sayings.

SPRING FORWARD!

Objective

Mathematics – To develop familiarity with the clock face and the changes we make in spring.

Group size

Whole group for introduction; groups of six.

What you need

Pictures showing daytime and night-time, a variety of clocks and watches, a large play clock, circular lids (make a needle hole in the centre), felt-tipped pens, strips of coloured card cut into shorter and longer clock hands, paper fasteners, small blackboard or white board with a large circle drawn on it.

Preparation

Gather the group and look at the pictures showing night-time and daytime together. Ask the children whether it is light or dark when they have their tea and when they go to bed. Explain that when spring comes we find a way of keeping it light for longer so that we can enjoy outdoor activities. Show the collection of clocks and watches. Use the play clock to explain how we move our clocks and watches one hour forward on a special night at the end of March.

What to do

Gather six children round the table and give each a prepared circular lid and a felt-tipped pen. Display the play clock so the children can see it clearly and discuss the numerals around the clock face. Using the small board with a large circle drawn on it, write the numerals one at a time. Assist the children in writing the numerals around their lids. Give each child two card hands (one large and one smaller) and a paper fastener and help them to fix them on their 'clocks'. Encourage the children to practise making their clocks show midnight – then move them on one hour.

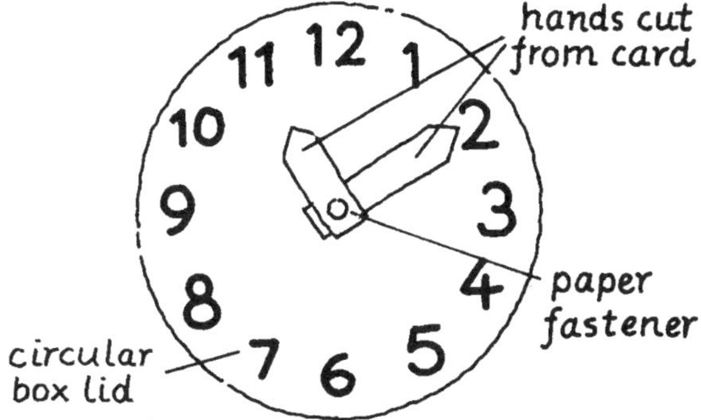

Discussion

Encourage the children to think of things they can enjoy doing in the daylight that they can't do in the dark such as playing outside, riding bikes or playing in the park. What is it like to go to bed in the light? Is it easier or harder to get to sleep? What are the things that grown-ups can do in the evenings when it is light that they cannot do in the dark? (Gardening, washing the car.) Would we still get more daylight each spring if we didn't change the clocks?

Follow-up activities

✧ Draw pictures of daytime activities on light paper and night-time ones on dark paper.
✧ Make a book of 'Things we can do on lighter evenings'.
✧ Set up a display table of different kinds of clocks and watches.
✧ Read the poem 'Winter to Spring' on page 71.

WARMER DAYS

Objective

Science – To find out about weather temperature and the need to wear different clothing.

Group size

Six to eight children.

What you need

An orange, a globe, two rubber hot-water bottles, a heavy woollen jumper, a cotton T-shirt, hot water.

Preparation

Place the objects on a table.

What to do

Gather the children on the carpet. Show them the globe and explain that this represents our planet 'earth' and point out some of the features such as seas, rivers, the North pole. Ask the children if they know where we live on earth, and point out the country. Hold the orange and tell the children that it represents the sun. Ask one of the group to hold the orange and show the children how the earth moves around the sun. Explain that the earth is nearer to the sun at different times which gives us our seasons.

Show the group the woolly jumper and the T-shirt. Ask the children to point out differences between them. Explain that in the autumn and winter we need warmer and thicker clothes, and that in spring and summer we need lighter and cooler clothes.

Fill the water bottles with hot water and, under supervision, allow the children to touch each bottle to show that they are the same temperature. Wrap one bottle in the T-shirt and the other in the woolly jumper. Explain that you are going to leave the bottles for a few hours to see what happens.

Later in the day bring the children back together and test to see which bottle is warmer.

Discussion

Ask the children if the sun is always in the sky. What seasons are sunny and warm? What is the weather like in winter? When do we wear clothes to keep us warm? What clothes help to keep us warm? What sort of clothes do we wear in warmer weather? Why do we have hot-water bottles? Is one bottle warmer than the other? Which one? Which top would you wear on a warm spring day?

Follow-up activities

✧ Make a collection of cool clothes for warm days and warm clothes for cold days.
✧ Let the children investigate places on the globe, picking out important features.

APRIL SHOWERS

Objective

Music – To listen carefully to sounds and to re-create them using voices, clapping and simple percussion instruments.

Group size

Various.

What you need

The poem 'Here comes the rain' on page 71, percussion instruments (triangles, tambourines, chime bars, claves), plastic sheet, a small watering can with a rose head, a metal bucket, a glass jar and a plastic bowl, water.

Preparation

On a rainy day take the children outdoors to listen to the rain. Stand in several shelters to show that rain sounds different in different places. Listen to and look at rain falling on the window panes. Back inside put down the plastic sheet on the carpet.

What to do

Group the children around the plastic sheet and remind them of their experiences of listening to the rain. Read the poem 'Here comes the rain' together and say it aloud several times, encouraging the children to enjoy the sounds of the words.

Fill the watering can with water and pour water into the containers (metal bucket, glass jar and plastic bowl). Ask the children to listen to the water as it's poured into the bowls. Pour at different speeds and point out the differences in the sounds they hear (soft, quiet, gentle, loud and so on).

Read the poem again and this time choose children to accompany the poem using their voices, clapping and the instruments.

Discussion

What sounds does the rain make? Why does it make different sounds as it falls? If you listen to the rain when you are indoors, does it sound the same as when you are outside? How can we make our voices sound like the rain? Which instrument sounds like a shower of rain? Which instrument can we use for heavy rainfall? Encourage the children to think about the differences between a rainy day and a showery day.

Follow-up activities

✧ Learn and dramatise the rhyme 'Doctor Foster'.
✧ Listen to small sections of 'Spring' from Vivaldi's *Four Seasons*. Ask the children which bits describe rain falling.
✧ Make a collection of rainy day things (umbrellas, wellington boots).
✧ Test different materials to see if they are rainproof.
✧ Carry out a weather survey and keep a record of wet days.

THE WEATHER BATTLE

Objective

English – To listen to a traditional story and respond by acting it out.

Group size

Any size.

What you need

A version of ***The North Wind and the Sun***, Aesops fable. A large space, a brightly patterned curtain, a hobby horse, sheets of thick blue and yellow card, felt-tipped pens, two bamboo canes, adhesive tape.

Preparation

Read the story ***The North Wind and the Sun***. Use a felt-tipped pen to draw a large swirly picture of a face on the blue card to represent the North Wind, and a spiky sun with a face on the yellow card. Cut these out and secure them to the bamboo canes with the adhesive tape. Pull the strings through the tape at both ends of the curtain so the top gathers to make a cape. Tie a knot at both ends to secure.

What to do

Take the book, props and children into a large space. Group the children on the carpet/floor and go over the sequences of the weather battle between the North Wind and the Sun. Show them the props and invite the children to dramatise the story. Choose children to play different parts (the North Wind, sun, horseman, people chasing their hat, people chatting, sailors being tossed on the sea, animals, birds, insects, trees). Help the children to act out the story, using simple sentences to structure their imaginative role play.

Discussion

Why did the North Wind and the Sun want to have a battle? What did the horseman do when the wind began to blow? Why were the animals frightened? Did the horseman take off his new cape? What happened when the sun began to shine? Why did the people come out? When did the horseman remove his cape? Who won the battle by warmth and gentleness? Discuss the weather changes in spring and encourage the children to recognise that springtime brings warmer weather but can also bring windy and showery weather too.

Follow-up activities

✧ Make a list of 'Things that happen on warm, sunny days' and 'Things that happen on windy days'.

✧ Read the poem 'Weatherwise' on page 67.

✧ Invite the children to write their own versions of the story.

✧ Emphasise the moral aspect of the story, telling children that it is better to be kind and gentle rather than strong and angry.

CALENDAR TIME

Objective

Mathematics – To learn about the concept of seasons and to match and sort items.

Group size

Up to six children.

What you need

A selection of pictures from old calendars showing different scenes at different times of the year (snow scenes, autumn trees, spring flowers, blossom, baby animals, holiday, summer scenes), a current scenic calendar, coloured card, felt-tipped pens.

Preparation

Mount the pictures onto separate pieces of card. Write the season on the back of each picture. Cut up coloured card to make labels.

What to do

Gather the children together and show them the calendar. Explain that it is made up of scenes for different times of the year. Point out that the year is made up of four seasons and the calendar pictures show things that happen in those seasons. Show the children a snowy picture and ask them whether it is a wintertime or summertime scene. Make a label saying 'winter' and place it near the snowy picture. Show the children the other pictures and ask them to decide which season is shown. Make labels for spring, summer and autumn. Go through other pictures and encourage the children to place the scenes in the correct seasonal set.

Discussion

Why do we use a calendar? How do people know which season it is? Encourage the children to repeat the season sequence. Which picture shows winter? How can we tell it is summer? What happens to the trees in autumn? What can we see in the spring picture?

Follow-up activities

✧ Extend the activity by giving the children a copy of the photocopiable sheet 'Odd one out' on page 88.
✧ Collect spring pictures from calendars and paste them onto thick card. Cut each picture into irregular shapes to make jigsaws. Let the children match the pieces of their springtime jigsaws.
✧ Play 'Guess my season' using the calendar pictures. Encourage the children to guess the season by describing what is in the picture.
✧ Collect some objects, pictures or photographs that relate to the seasons. Ask the children to sort them into the appropriate sets.

THE SELFISH GIANT

Objective

RE – To develop awareness of selfishness and the consequences of this behaviour.

Group size

Whole class or large group.

What you need

The story of 'The selfish giant' on page 86. Large sheets of pale grey and bright blue card, sheets of green and white paper, glue sticks, silver glitter, pictures of trees and shrubs in winter and spring, pictures of spring flowers, felt-tipped pens, pencils, coloured crayons, piece of white card, an easel or board.

Preparation

Use the white paper to cut out a snowy landscape, place it on the green paper and copy the outline. Cut along the outlines. Place the white landscape onto the pale grey card and glue it down. Repeat this with the green paper and blue card. Draw a fence around the winter garden. Cut pictures of shrubs, trees and flowers to appropriate sizes and a sign for the winter garden. Write captions.

What to do

Read the story of 'The selfish giant'. Emphasise the point that the giant was selfish because he did not want to share his beautiful garden.

Secure the winter scene to an easel or board, show the children the sign and explain the message. Encourage the children to think and discuss what the garden would be like in winter. Ask some children to choose a suitable picture and stick it onto the scene. Sprinkle silver glitter onto the trees to represent frost.

Remove the winter garden from the easel or board and pin up the spring garden landscape. Recap the part of the story where the giant helps the little boy into the tree. Glue one of the winter tree pictures onto the garden scene. Ask several children to choose trees, flowers and shrubs and glue these on.

Arrange the children into groups and ask them to draw themselves playing in the giant's garden. Place the picture of the happy giant standing in his garden. Mount and display the two scenes with the children's own pictures and let them retell the story.

Discussion

Tell the children that many stories teach us how to behave and think of other people. Why didn't spring come into the selfish giant's garden? What was singing in the giant's garden? What did the giant see? Why did the giant help the little boy? Do you think the giant liked to see the signs of spring in his garden? Was the giant selfish any more?

Follow-up activities

✧ Talk about the way in which the children can be kind to each other.
✧ Sing the song 'Could this be a sign?' from *Spring Tinderbox* (A & C Black).

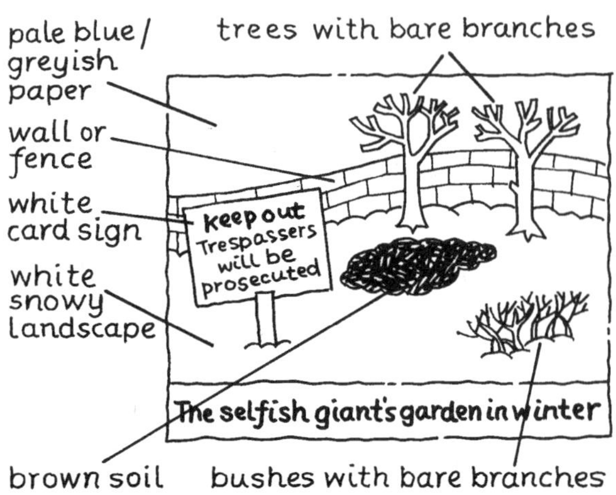

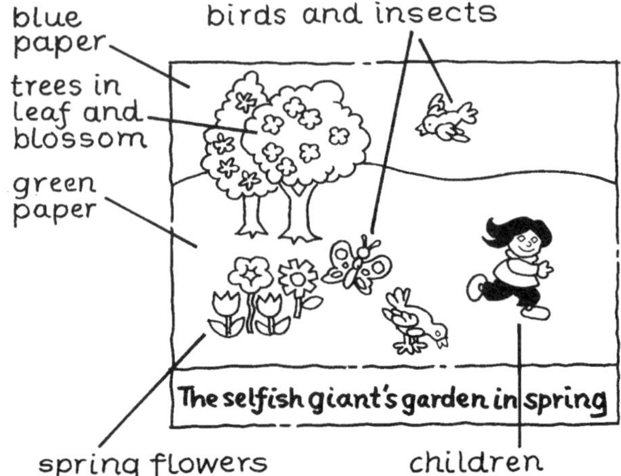

SPRING BARGAINS

Objective

Art – To create a shop window of clothes for spring, using a variety of media.

Group size

Six to eight children.

What you need

A large area of wall space, backing paper, strips of dark card, grey/buff sugar paper, paints, felt-tipped pens, crayons, brightly coloured and patterned fabric, a selection of buttons (different sizes, colours and shapes), pieces of ribbon and lace, scissors, strong adhesive, glue spreaders, a catalogue showing spring clothing, assorted waste boxes, plastic cloth, aprons.

Preparation

Prepare the display area by covering it with backing paper. Cut card into narrow strips to make the shop window. Prepare the activity table. Set out the different media. Cut sugar paper and fabric into appropriate sizes for children to cut out different shapes. Cut a large piece of card for the shop name.

What to do

Gather the children on the carpet and show them the spring catalogue. Point out that the clothes are light-weight clothing designed for wearing in the warmer weather. Discuss the idea of making a shop window showing a display of clothes for spring. Invite the children to make clothes for the window display.

Take the group to the activity table and make sure each child wears an apron. Encourage the children to cut out different clothes shapes and to decorate them using the different media. Invite them to suggest where they should be placed on the display board. Secure the waste boxes to the display. Attach some of the clothes to the boxes to give a 3D effect.

Invite the children to choose a name for the shop. Write a large label and put it above the shop window. Write captions saying 'Buy new spring clothes here' and 'Best bargains in town'.

Discussion

What kind of clothes do we wear in the spring? Invite the children to share their experiences of shopping for new clothes. How can we make the clothes? Why do shops put clothes in the window? How shall we display them in the shop window? What labels shall we put near our clothes? What shall we call the shop?

Follow-up activities

✧ Design and make catalogues for the shop showing clothes, descriptions, sizes and prices.
✧ Dress dolls and teddies in new spring fashions.
✧ Organise a fashion show and invite children to wear spring clothes.

WEATHER REPORT

Objective

Science – To learn some weather sayings and to find out about weather forecasting.

Group size

Up to four children.

What you need

A large map of the British Isles, a small table, pieces of thin card, Blu-Tack, large scissors, coloured felt-tipped pens, coloured crayons, pieces of white card, pieces of coloured card, an easel or board.

Preparation

Cut pictures out of card to represent clouds, wind, sun, fog, frost, showers and rain. Colour in as appropriate to represent each type of weather. Stick a small piece of Blu-Tack on the back of each symbol. Attach the map to the easel or board. Write captions for the following sayings: 'April showers bring forth May flowers', 'Fog in March, frost in May', 'March comes in like a lion, goes out like a lamb' 'February fills the dykes', 'If the oak is before the ash then we're in for quite a splash but if the ash is before the oak then we're in for quite a soak'.

What to do

Gather the children around the easel or display board and tell them that there can be different types of weather in springtime. Explain that there are many weather sayings and some are about the spring months. Read the captions to the children and explain what they mean.

Ask the children if they have seen weather reports on the television. Show the symbols and invite the children to suggest what each one represents. Point to the map and encourage the children to do a weather report for the day. Invite the children to take turns to be the weather person.

Discussion

Tell the children that a long time ago, people looked at signs in the countryside to forecast the weather. How do we know what the weather is going to be like? (Radio, television, newspapers, looking at the sky.) What do the weather people do on the television reports? (Point to different parts of the country, add or point out the weather symbols.) What do the symbols tell us? Are the weather forecasts always right?

Follow-up activities

✧ Ask the children to listen to or watch a weather forecast at home and compare what you all heard or saw.
✧ Find more weather sayings for different times of the year.
✧ Keep a record of the weather for one week.
✧ Learn songs and nursery rhymes that refer to the weather (Doctor Foster, The North Wind doth blow, Rock-a-bye baby).

CHAPTER 2 OUTDOOR SIGNS OF SPRING

Make use of the extra daytime to explore the great outdoors with simple observations of spring growth in the park, among the hedgerows and at the pond.

OFF TO THE PARK

Objective

Geography – To undertake a simple observation task.

Group size

Whole group for the introduction. Groups of six, accompanied by an adult, for the walk and the observation task.

What you need

An easel with a large sheet marked 'Things we found in the park' pinned to it, clipboards with a copy of photocopiable page 89 attatched to it for each group, a pencil, an adult helper for each group, a camera (optional).

Preparation

Photocopy page 89, sufficient for one per group. Explain to the children that as it is a fine day you are all going for a walk to the park to look for signs of spring. Point out the items on the sheet and explain that each group will have a copy so that they will remember what they are going to look for.

What to do

Divide the children into groups of six, each with a well-briefed adult helper. Once in the park remind the children what they are looking for and allow the groups to disperse. Arrange a re-assembly point and allow about fifteen minutes for the task. If possible take some photographs of the children and the wildlife.

Back at your group base, transfer the findings to the large sheet on the easel. Encourage the children to contribute their comments on what they saw on the walk.

Discussion

What signs of spring can we see in the park? Encourage the children to name the items on the sheet. Where did we find them? Were there any items that we didn't find? Why was this? Encourage the children to explain what will happen next to the green shoots. What other signs of spring did we see? If we visit the park in a few weeks time will the flowers still look the same?

Follow-up activities

✧ Play 'The park game' on photocopiable page 90.
✧ Make observational drawings of the wildlife seen in the park, using different media.
✧ Mount the observation sheets, the children's drawings and some photographs to form a display.
✧ Make a table-top display showing items found in the park (crocus, catkins, daffodils) and other items not found, for example a tin of beans, a clothes-peg, a sock. Encourage the children to identify the items seen on their walk.
✧ Read the poem 'I like the park' on page 68.

IN THE HEDGEROW

Objective

Science – To observe that warmth and light encourage the growth of blossoms and leaves.

Group size

Any size.

What you need

A selection of things that grow in the hedge such as hawthorn, forsythia, kerria or any other flowering shrubs. Several large jars, water, access to a warm, light area (such as a window ledge), an accessible cool, sheltered, outdoor spot.

Preparation

In early spring take the children for a walk to an area where they can see hedges and bushes (local park, neighbouring gardens, waste land, natural conservation area). Point out the 'winter state' of the hedges and shrubs. Explain that some hedges keep their green leaves all winter but many lose their greenness and must wait until the warmer days arrive to grow again. Choose a selection of different twigs which are coming into bud.

What to do

Remind the children of the walk and show them the twigs. Explain that the twigs have been brought into the warm to trick them into thinking it is time for summer. Tell the children the names of the twigs.

Ask a child to place the twigs in the jars. Place some jars in the warm, sunny spot indoors, and the others in the cool, shady place outside. Ask the children to look daily at both sets of twigs to see what happens. Encourage the children to talk about the changes they can see to the different twigs.

Discussion

Ask the children to describe the hedgerows they saw on the walk. Did all the hedges lose their leaves in winter? Why are we tricking the twigs to think it is nearer summer? What would happen if we did not put the twigs in water? How do the hedgerows get water? What will happen to the twigs that stay in the warm room? Will the same happen to the twigs that are kept outside? What changes can we see? Why do the indoor twigs come into leaf and blossom first?

Follow-up activities

✧ Make observational drawings of the twigs at different stages.
✧ Learn the song 'Spring blossom' on page 74.
✧ Investigate other life in the hedgerows such as insects, birds, small animals.

SPRING FLOWERS

Objective

Art – To develop observation of colour, shape and texture and to make 3D examples.

Group size

Up to six children.

What you need

Pictures of daffodils, some fully developed daffodils with leaves, jars of water, scissors, yellow tissue paper, yellow and green fabric of different kinds, egg boxes, paint in bright and pale yellow, orange, and dark and light green. Strong adhesive, spreaders, green gummed paper, thin white card, blue and green frieze paper, pieces of sponge, newspaper or plastic cloth, aprons.

Preparation

Prepare the frieze board by placing blue and green frieze paper to represent the sky and ground. Cut up the egg boxes and separate 'nests'. Cover the table with newspaper or plastic cloth. Put the rest of the materials on the table. Place the daffodils in a jar.

What to do

Gather the children around the prepared table and show the children the daffodil pictures and real blooms. Tell the children the names of the different parts (trumpet, petals, stem, leaves). Allow the children to touch and smell the different parts of the daffodils.

Invite two or three children to design a background using sponge printing for the display board. Point out the different materials available and ask the children which materials would be suitable to represent the parts of the daffodil.

Invite children to make their own daffodils on the thin card. Move around the group giving support where necessary. Wait for the background prints and the children's individual daffodils to dry. Encourage the children to place their completed daffodils on the frieze.

Discussion

What colour are daffodils? What else is yellow? What is the frilly part in the middle called? Do the petals and leaves feel the same? Ask the children to describe the stems and leaves. Where do daffodils grow? What happens if you squeeze the bottom of the stem? Why do we give daffodils water? Do daffodils grow from seeds or bulbs? Explain that daffodil bulbs can be planted indoors in the winter so we have flowers early in the year.

Follow-up activities

✧ Read the poem 'Trumpet of Spring' on page 71.

✧ Set up a yellow and gold display table and encourage the children to collect interesting objects.

✧ Bring in some examples of other spring flowers (tulips, crocus, snowdrops) and make a graph to show the children's favourites.

✧ Sing the song 'Daffodil' on page 74.

CHANGES EVERYWHERE!

Objective

English – To develop thinking and sequencing skills.

Group size

Up to four children.

What you need

Photographs and pictures of: eggs, chickens, hens, bulb, bulb with leaves, daffodil or tulip, frogspawn, tadpoles, frogs, caterpillar eggs, caterpillar, cocoon, butterfly, bare tree, tree with buds, tree with leaves, seed, stem and leaves, beans or sunflower, baby lambs and sheep. Scissors, thick card, adhesive film.

Preparation

Cut out the pictures or photographs and mount them on card. Cover with adhesive plastic film. Cut around the pictures to make individual cards.

What to do

Gather the children together around a table. Draw their attention to the cards and encourage them to say what the cards show. It is important that the children recognise all the objects on the cards. Remind the children that spring is a special time – animals have new babies, creatures come out of hibernation, flowers start to grow, the days get longer and warmer. Explain that the cards show what happens to some of the creatures and plants during the spring.

Pick up the card of the egg. Invite the children to suggest what happens next. Go through the cards asking, 'Does this happen next?' until they choose the chicken card. Place the chicken card next to the egg card. Carry on with this sequencing until all the cards are displayed on the table.

Suggest the children play a game called 'What happens next?'. Place all the cards in the middle of the table with pictures face down. Invite one child to take a card and place it in the middle of the table. Each child takes a card in turn. If it shows 'what happens next' it is placed next to the first card. If it does not, it is placed back on the table. The child who places the last of the sequence wins. Repeat until all cards are collected in sequence.

Discussion

Why is spring such a special time? What changes do we see in the spring? Where do we find frogspawn? What happens next to the tadpole? What comes before the daffodil? Where does the butterfly come from?

Follow-up activities

✧ Talk about other activities with which the children are familiar, for example getting dressed, pouring a fizzy drink, eating a banana, blowing up a balloon.
✧ Give the children the photocopiable sheet 'What happens next?' on page 90 and ask them to draw the pictures to show what happens next.
✧ Read the story 'Boing! Boing! Boing!' on page 83.
✧ Learn the poem ' Wake up' on page 70.

AT THE POND

Objective

Science – To develop understanding of pond life in spring and to reinforce positional language.

Group size

Six children.

What you need

Different coloured card, pictures of creatures (frog, newt, ram's-horn snail, water beetle, water flea, perch, dragonfly), birds (heron, moorhen, mallard) and plants (bulrush, water lily, water iris), a large piece of blue fabric or felt, a selection of green fabric, adhesive, a child's fishing net, white card, felt-tipped pens.

Preparation

Cut out the pictures and stick them onto the card. Cut the blue fabric into a pond shape. Cut strands of green to form reeds at the edge of the pond. Cut the handle of the fishing net short so that children can handle it easily. Write labels saying 'in the pond', 'by the pond', 'above the pond'.

What to do

Ideally, start by arranging a visit to a pond to observe pond life.

Gather the children together and talk about pond life in spring. Explain that the creatures who have been sleeping at the bottom of the pond during the winter, begin to wake up and are ready to lay their eggs. Show the children the pictures and tell them what they show. Ask the children if they think the creatures live by the pond, in the pond or above the pond. Carry out the same process with the birds and plants.

Show the children the fishing net, and invite them to dip it into the 'pond'. Put the cards into the net and remove one at a time using the net. Ask the children to identify the creature, bird or plant they pick up and suggest where it should be placed (by the pond, in the pond or above the pond). When all the cards have been used, show the children the labels and place them in the correct place.

Discussion

What happens to the pond creatures in spring? Why do the creatures come to the top of the pond? Who lays her eggs in the reeds by the pond? Explain that some creatures can go both in the pond and by the pond (frogs, newts). Where do fish lay their eggs? Ask the children to name the creatures, birds and plants. What happens to the plants by the side of the pond in spring?

Follow-up activities

✧ Sort the pictures into different sets: those that can swim, those that are green, those that come to the pond and those that live in the pond.

✧ Play the game 'Guess my name'. Choose a card, describe the creature, bird or plant and invite the children to guess what it is.

✧ Sing the song 'I'm a frog' on page 75.

LET'S PLAY TADPOLES

Objective

PE – To develop understanding of team games and introduce simple rules and instructions.

Group size

Whole class or large group.

What you need

A large outdoor play area, chalk, a soft ball, two small chairs, a beanbag, some chalk, a chalkboard, a collection of small PE apparatus (bats, balls, skipping ropes), an adult helper.

Preparation

Draw a large circle on the ground with a long, straight line alongside it, using the chalk. Place the chairs nearby. Collect together the small apparatus.

What to do

Gather the children together and explain that in springtime the days are warmer and longer and they can play outside. Tell the children they are going to learn a new game called 'Tadpoles'. Divide the group into two, one will be the tadpole's tail and the other its body. Draw this diagram on the chalkboard:

Tail group – Arrange the children along the line. Give a beanbag to the first child. When the adult leader shouts 'Go', the first child runs and touches the first and second chair with the beanbag. He/she goes back to his/her place in the line and gives the beanbag to the next child. When each child has completed the running and returned to the line they shout 'Tadpole'.

Body group – Organise the children into a circle around the drawn 'body'. The adult helper stands in the middle holding the ball. When the adult leader shouts 'Go', the helper throws the ball to each child in turn. The group can count each catch. Everyone stops when the 'tail' group shout 'Tadpole'. The two groups exchange places.

Discussion

Talk about different games that are played outside. What games do you like to play? Explain that some of the games they play are very old (hopscotch, marbles, skipping, hide-and-seek) and some are newer games which they make up. What did the 'body' group have to do in the game? How many catches did you count? Which part of the game did you like best? Why?

Follow-up activities

✧ Make a graph to show the children's favourite games.
✧ Find out about some traditional games and learn some of them; ask parents and grandparents to share their memories of games.

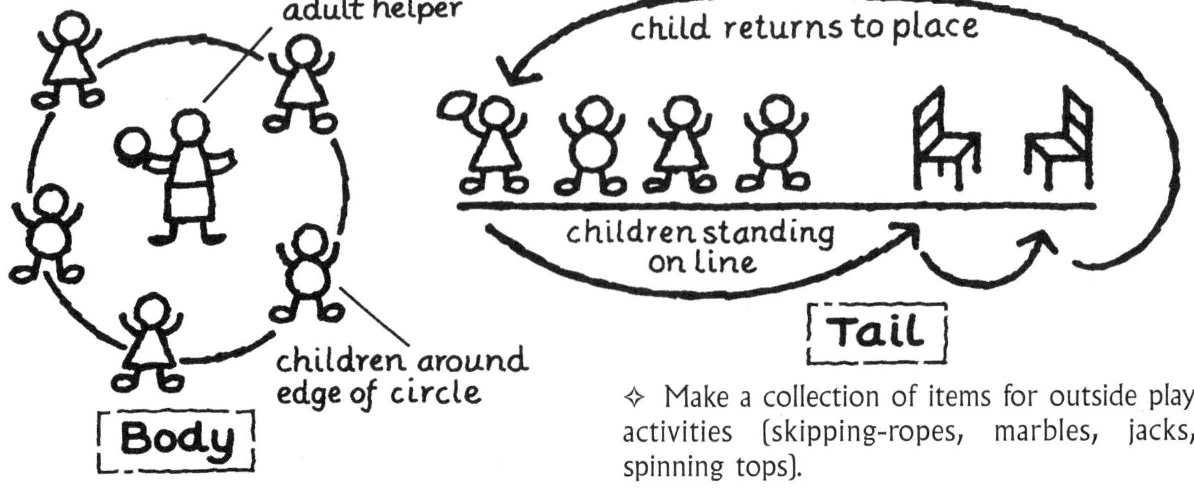

✧ Make a collection of items for outside play activities (skipping-ropes, marbles, jacks, spinning tops).

IN THE GARDEN

Objective

English – To develop speaking and listening skills.

Group size

Any size.

What you need

A selection of garden objects (trowel, garden cane, a plant label, watering can, seeds, a bulb, a plant pot, some potting compost) and a selection of objects you would not find in a garden (hot water bottle, a bar of soap, a wooden spoon, a bag of flour, light bulb, a greeting card). A large cardboard box, a large piece of green fabric or curtain, the nursery rhyme 'Mary, Mary, quite contrary'.

Preparation

Teach the children the nursery rhyme 'Mary, Mary, quite contrary'. Assemble all the objects into the cardboard box. Place the green fabric or curtain on the top.

What to do

Gather the children into a space and sing 'Mary, Mary, quite contrary' together. Ask the children to think about the things Mary had growing in her garden (silver bells, cockle shells, pretty maids). Explain that spring is a busy time for gardeners as it's a time for planting seeds and plants that will grow into fruit, flowers and vegetables to be enjoyed later in the year.

Unfold the green fabric and ask the children to imagine that it is a part of a garden. Tell them that inside the box are some things that might be found in the garden and some that are not. Invite the children to discover what objects belong in the garden and suggest that they place these objects on the green fabric. Things which do not belong in the garden should be placed outside the green fabric.

Invite individual children to pick an object out of the box and encourage the group to say what it is and how it is used. Invite the child to decide whether it should go 'in the garden' or 'out of the garden'.

Discussion

What did Mary have in her garden? Do you usually see these in the garden? What kinds of things do we see? Why is spring a busy time in the garden? Where do seeds and bulbs need to go? Why do things start to grow in the spring? What do gardeners need to help do the gardening? Do seeds grow into vegetables straight away? What other things might you see in a garden?

Follow-up activities

✧ Read the story of *Jasper's Beanstalk* by Nick Butterworth and Mick Inkpen (Hodder Children's Books).
✧ Grow different seeds (beans, peas, cress) and observe/record their different rates of growth.
✧ Cut out stencils of spring words, and sow mustard and cress onto damp cotton wool or kitchen towel to grow in the word shapes.
✧ Read the poem 'Seed needs' on page 72.

SING WHAT WE SEE

Objective

Music – To sing a song from memory.

Group size

Any size.

What you need

Pictures or objects showing some of the outdoor signs of spring (sticky buds, twigs sprouting new leaves, hazel catkins, violets), a small table or cupboard top, fabric drape, scissors, pieces of card.

Preparation

Cut out the spring pictures and mount them onto thick card. Cover the table or cupboard top with the fabric drape. Place the objects on the display area.

What to do

Show the children the pictures and objects pointing out the signs of spring that can be seen outdoors. Hum the tune, 'What shall we do with the drunken sailor?'. Tell the children that they are going to use that special tune to learn a song about outdoor signs of spring. Sing the following song and pick up the appropriate objects to reinforce the words:

Chorus (after each verse)
What do we see in the countryside? (twice)
What do we see in the countryside now that springtime's here?

1. Hedges sprouting new green leaves (twice)
   That's a sign spring's here.
2. Catkins looking like lambs' tails (twice)
   That's a sign spring's here.
3. Purple violets in the hedgerow (twice)
   That's a sign spring's here.
4. Sticky buds bursting open (twice)
   That's a sign spring's here.
5. These are outdoor signs of spring (twice)
   Spring is here again!

Discussion

What signs of spring do we see outdoors? What other signs could we add to our song? (Primroses, pussy willows, birds nesting, animals waking up from hibernation.) Why do leaves appear in spring? Why do catkins remind us of lambs' tails? What are the colours of spring flowers?

Follow-up activities

✧ Look in information books about the outdoor signs of spring.
✧ Encourage the children to add their own ideas to the song.
✧ Add percussion instruments to accompany the singing.
✧ Listen to other songs written about spring (see pages 73 to 80.)

CHAPTER 3 SPRING TRADITIONS

Spring heralds the arrival of many special festivals and traditions including Mothering Sunday, Easter and May Day. Ideas in this chapter include activities to cook, make cards and dance around a maypole.

MOTHERING SUNDAY

Objective

History – To develop awareness of historical traditions.

Group size

Whole group for introduction, then groups of four.

What you need

Large pieces of coloured card, some Mother's Day cards, old seed and gardening catalogues, adhesive sticks, small pieces of coloured ribbon, felt-tipped pens, pencils, scissors, newspaper or plastic cloth, aprons, pictures of servants from Victorian and Edwardian houses.

Preparation

Cut card and fold to form gift cards. Cut out a selection of flower pictures from the catalogues and magazines. Cut the ribbon into pieces and make small bows. Cover the table and place all materials and aprons on it.

What to do

Throughout this activity make sure you are sensitive to individual family circumstances.

Gather the children together and show them the Mother's Day cards. Ask the children if they know why there is a special day for mothers. Explain that many years ago, some girls went to be servants in big houses. Show the pictures of the servants and invite the children to say what is happening. Tell the children that servant girls were only allowed home to see their mothers on one Sunday in spring and they picked posies of wild flowers to take home as a present. Refer to the present celebration of Mother's Day.

Invite the children to make a special flower card for their mothers to remind them of the servant girls long ago. Show the children the materials available.

Allow each child to make a posy of flowers on the 'Mother's Day' card using the pictures from magazines. Demonstrate how to add stems using the felt-tipped pens. Complete by choosing bows to stick onto the posies. Write the caption 'Happy Mother's Day, With love from' inside the card and get the children to add their own names.

Discussion

Encourage the children to think about life as a servant girl in a large house. What would they wear? Who looked after them (washed and ironed their clothes, cooked their meals)? How did they show their mothers that they loved them? Why couldn't the servant girls telephone home or write letters? Ask the children if they do special things for their mothers (give cards and presents, help with jobs).

Follow-up activities

✧ Arrange a visit to a museum or house which has a 'Victorian' kitchen.
✧ Find out about the origins of Simnel cake.
✧ Encourage the children to draw and paint their own 'servant girl' pictures.

PANCAKE DAY

Objective

Technology – To cook pancakes and explore different tastes.

Group size

Whole group for introduction, then groups of four.

What you need

A plastic tablecloth, aprons, kitchen roll, plain flour, milk, one egg, a pinch of salt, fat for frying, castor sugar, jam, oranges, golden syrup, lemons. Large and small basin, half-pint measuring jug, metal and wooden spoon, flat egg whisk, small frying pan, wooden spatula, cooker or hotplate, paper plates, teaspoons, a board or easel, two sheets of large white paper, two pegs, a felt-tipped pen.

Preparation

Cover the table with the plastic tablecloth and set out the aprons, ingredients and cooking utensils. Cut the oranges and lemons into halves. Secure the paper to the easel or board. Write a heading 'Toppings for pancakes' and list the toppings being used. On another large piece of paper write the captions, 'Our favourite topping' and 'Our least favourite topping'.

What to do

Gather the children around the table and show them the ingredients and utensils, naming them one by one. Invite a child to measure four rounded tablespoons of flour out into the basin. Encourage individual children to whisk the egg, measure the milk and combine the egg, milk and flour. Take the frying pan, add fat and place on heat. Carefully allow each child to pour in enough batter for a pancake.

Turn or (if brave) toss the pancakes! Make enough pancakes to add the chosen toppings (sugar, lemon juice, orange juice, jam, golden syrup). Place the pancakes on plates.

Ask each child to choose a topping and put it onto a pancake. Cut up the pancakes and

invite the children to taste the different toppings. Carry out a quick survey to find each child's favourite and least favourite topping. Make a list showing the children's favourite and least favourite toppings.

Discussion

Tell the children that there is a special time before Easter called Lent, which originally meant spring. Christians think of the time Jesus was praying in the wilderness. During Lent, Christians gave up eating rich foods. On the day before Lent (Shrove Tuesday), people would say sorry for things they had done wrong. They would have a feast of pancakes to use up all the rich food (for example fat, eggs, meat) before the 'fast' started. Ask the children if they would give up anything special during this time. What special treats would they miss? Encourage the children to think about people who are hungry. What name is given to the mixture? What would happen if we added too much milk? How are pancakes cooked? What other toppings could you try?

Follow-up activities

✧ Organise a parents' pancake race with sponsorship for charity.
✧ Take photographs of the pancake-making. Ask the children to place the photographs in sequence.
✧ Learn 'Mix a pancake' from ***Harlequin – 44 songs round the year*** (A & C Black).
✧ Find out about other Mardi Gras festivals held in other countries.
✧ Learn the song 'Pancakes' in the Resources section on page 78.

SPRING BANK HOLIDAY

Objective

Art – To use different media to create a journey to the seaside.

Group size

Small groups.

What you need

Topsy and Tim Go on Holiday by Jean and Gareth Anderson (Puffin Books). A large display board, white and coloured card, felt-tipped pens, pencils, crayons, coloured backing paper, poster paints, paintbrushes, adhesive, glue spreaders, aprons, newspaper, scissors, fabric scraps, coloured paper, sponges, other media for printing (rag, different kinds of paper, potatoes), adult helpers.

Preparation

Divide the display board into four sections. Cover with different coloured backing paper. Write large captions saying 'Getting ready', 'On the way', A picnic lunch', 'At the seaside'. Cover the tables with newspaper. Place the different media and appropriate equipment on each table (painting, printing, colouring, collage). Read *Topsy and Tim Go on Holiday.*

What to do

Show the children the four display boards and read the captions. Recap on the story and suggest that groups of children work on each part of the story.

The group activities should comprise: preparing for the outing, the journey in the car, having a picnic lunch, having fun at the seaside.

Invite the children to suggest what might be included in the sections (preparing the picnic, packing the car, putting on appropriate outfits, eating the picnic lunch and playing on the beach). Organise the materials so that different media is available to include painting, collage, printing and drawing. Set each group to work at a table and assign an adult to supervise each group. Go round each group offering support

and encouraging them to reflect on their own experiences. When the work is ready, allow the children to choose on which section of the display board they will place their work, until the display is complete.

Discussion

Why do we have Spring Bank Holiday? Where did Topsy and Tim go? What preparations did Mum and Dad make? Ask the children what they would take to the seaside. How could you travel? Encourage the children to describe what they would see on the journey. Explain that on long journeys we might need to stop for a break. Where might you stop for a picnic lunch? What would you have on a picnic? Ask the children what things you can do at the seaside. Encourage the children to decide what they are going to put in each section of the display. How could we represent the sea? What else would you see at the seaside?

Follow-up activities

✧ Carry out a survey to find out what children did on Spring Bank Holiday.
✧ Set up the role play area as a travel agent. Include posters and brochures for day trips by coach, car and train.
✧ Make a book about 'Special days out'.
✧ Learn the song 'It's Bank Holiday Monday' on page 77.

HAT PARADE

Objective

Design and Technology – To look at different designs of hats and then design one.

Group size

Up to six children at a time.

What you need

A selection of children's and adults' hats suitable for warmer weather and special occasions (a bobble hat, a straw boater, a trilby, a top hat, a beret). Old magazines, crayons, paints, felt-tipped pens, adhesive, a selection of brightly coloured feathers, artificial flowers, crêpe paper, thick cardboard, brightly coloured card, scissors.

Preparation

Collect a selection of different hats. Cut out pictures of people wearing hats for different occasions from magazines. Make several templates of different shaped hats and use them to cut a selection of hats out of the brightly coloured card, varying the shape. Provide enough hats to give the children a choice of style and colour. Make some examples to show to the children.

What to do

Show the children the selection of hats. Ask them to identify who might wear each hat and when it might be worn (for a wedding, in cold weather, at the seaside). Explain that people wear hats at different times, to protect them from the weather, for safety, for fun and at special times of the year.

Show the children the hats you have made. Invite the children to select some of the materials to make a special hat for the 'Grand spring hat parade'.

When the hats are finished, gather all the children together. Encourage each child to model their hat and describe the materials they have used to make it. When all the children have designed their hats, organise a hat parade. Set up a hat display and include the children's designs. Write a caption: 'Our grand spring hat parade'.

Discussion

Why do people wear hats on special occasions? What sorts of hats do they wear? What different types of hats have you seen or do you have? Explain that people like to wear something new at this time of year to celebrate spring. Sometimes people join together in a parade to show off their new things, for example the Easter parade in New York. Suggest that the children show their new hats in a special hat parade.

Follow-up activities

✧ Read the poem 'The new spring hat' on page 67.
✧ Fill up some hats and find out how much they will hold (building bricks, teddies, beanbags).
✧ Collect pictures of different hats from magazines. Cut them into halves and stick onto thick card. Get the children to match the hats.
✧ Introduce different hats into the role play area (pirate's hat, top hat, bonnet, beret).

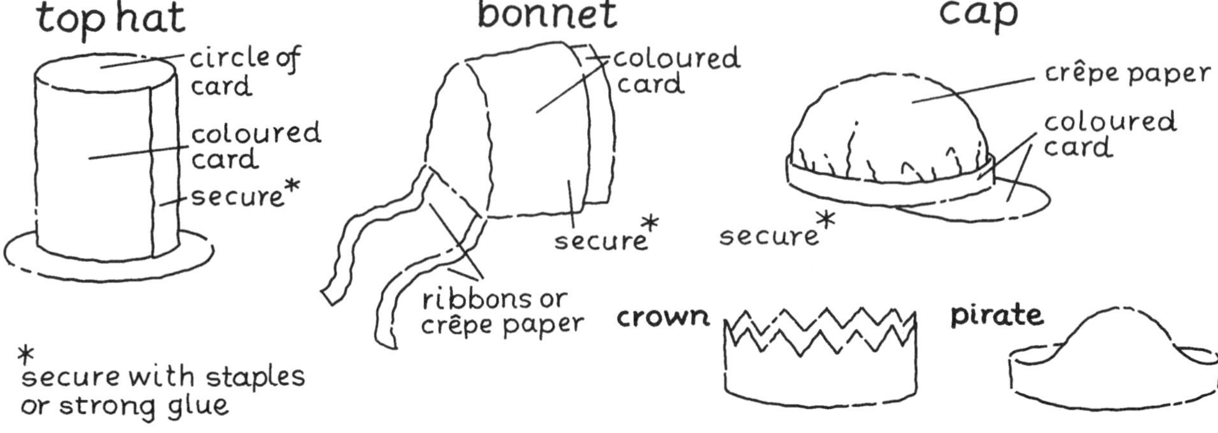

SPRING FAIRS

Objective

History – To learn about the differences between present day spring fairs and those in the past.

Group size

Up to six children.

What you need

Picture of present day fair, large pieces of stiff card, felt-tipped pens, lengths of wool or tape, hole punch, shepherd's crook, feather duster, wooden spoon, gardening trowel, butter or cheese, hammer and nails.

Preparation

Cut the card into six pieces (about 25cm × 10cm). Punch a hole in the top two corners. Cut wool or tape into lengths of 60cm. Insert wool or tape through both holes making a loop large enough to go over a child's head. Write 'shepherd', housemaid', 'cook', 'gardener', 'dairy maid' and 'carpenter' on one side of the six labels. Assemble the objects. Place the labels, objects and picture of the fair on a table.

What to do

Gather the children on the carpet and show them the picture of the fair. Ask if any of the children have been to a fair. Explain that the fairs we see and enjoy today are very different from fairs held a long time ago.

Explain that spring was a special time for fairs and people visited them to sell farm animals, vegetables, dairy foods, eggs, baskets, rugs and other things they had made or grown. It was also the time when people began to think about all the work that would be needed on farms and in big houses in the countryside. People would travel on foot to the fairs to find work. They would make labels to place around their necks and draw pictures to show people what kind of work they were looking for.

Point out the objects and encourage the children to suggest who might use each one in their work (for example, mop – housemaid, crook – shepherd). Invite each child to choose a label, place it over their head and read each label in turn. Encourage the children to then pick the object suited to their role and invite them to describe what they can do with the item.

Discussion

What do you see at the fair? Can you describe the stalls, games and other amusements? Explain that 'mop fairs' are held in some town streets today. Special permission was given to allow fairs in the street for a few days every year. Do people still travel to fairs to find work? How did people know what jobs these people could do?

Follow-up activities

✧ Extend the activity by giving the children the photocopiable sheet 'What do I use?' on page 91. Talk about the different people and objects shown on the sheet. Ask the children to draw a line to match the correct object to each person.

✧ Learn the traditional rhyme 'Oh dear what can the matter be?'.

✧ Write a group story called 'Fun at the fair'.

MAY DAY

Objective

History – To find out how people celebrated the coming of spring in the past.

Group size

Any size.

What you need

A large space, a tall pole, long pieces of coloured ribbon, staple gun, staples, needle, cotton, artificial flowers, a selection of dressing up clothes (long skirts, mop caps, baseball caps, straw or felt hats, braces), piece of gold card, children's baskets, two large chairs, old curtains, copy of the nursery rhyme 'Here we come gathering nuts in May'.

Preparation

Teach the children the nursery rhyme 'Here we come gathering nuts in May'. Place the pole firmly in the ground, attach the ribbon to the top and secure it with staples. Place the artificial flowers around the hats and sew them on to secure. Cut one edge of the gold card to represent a crown. Shape it to fit a child's head and fasten with staples. Place the chairs near the 'maypole' and cover with curtains to represent thrones. Place flowers in the baskets.

What to do

Gather the children together. Explain that people in towns and the country celebrated the beginning of spring by holding May Day festivals. A May King and Queen were chosen and people gave them spring flowers. People danced around a special pole called the 'maypole'.

Ask two children to be May King and Queen. Place the crowns on their heads and ask them to sit on the thrones. Encourage the other children to dress up. Ask boys to tuck long trousers into socks, put on the braces and give out the decorated hats. Girls can wear long dresses or skirts and carry the baskets of flowers.

Invite the children to give the flowers to the May King and Queen. Encourage them to bow or curtsey. Suggest the King and Queen start the festivities by saying 'Let the dancing begin'. Ask three boys and three girls to form a circle around the maypole. Give each child a ribbon and then encourage them to skip around the maypole. Invite the other children to sing 'Here we come gathering nuts in May'. Finish the festival with a procession around the space.

Discussion

Explain that the May King and Queen were chosen from the people. They were special for that May Day. Why were people glad that spring had arrived? What flowers would there be in May? How did people decorate the maypole? What happens to the ribbons as the dancers skip around the maypole? Have you ever seen people dancing around a maypole?

Follow-up activities

✧ Observe and record pictorially flowers that grow in the garden and in the wild during the month of May.
✧ Show the children pictures of Morris dancers and point out their costumes.
✧ Display information books about spring and encourage the children to look up spring festivals.
✧ Learn the song 'Maypole' on page 76.

ORANGES AND LEMONS

Objective

Music – To sing a traditional nursery rhyme and singing game.

Group size

Any size.

What you need

An orange, a lemon, a sharp knife, lemon squeezer, two small beakers, a cassette with the nursery rhyme 'Oranges and lemons'.

Preparation

Set up the cassette player. Cover the table and place the fruit and equipment on it.

What to do

Gather the whole group together. Ask the children if they can identify the fruit. Encourage them to describe the differences between oranges and lemons (shape, colour, taste). Get a couple of children to feel and smell the fruit. Invite them to describe how the fruit feels and smells. Cut the fruit into halves and show the children the insides. Squeeze the fruit juice into the beakers and show them the different juices.

Tell the children there is a famous song about oranges and lemons and play the cassette tape of the song 'Oranges and lemons'. Explain that the song was written many years ago and describes what happened when oranges and lemons were brought to London by sailing ships. Explain that St Clement's is a church near the River Thames. Porters carrying the oranges and lemons had to pay five farthings to pass through the buildings (Clement's Inn) to get to

Clare market, where they sold their fruit. Play the song again and invite children to join in.

Discussion

Does an orange taste the same as a lemon? What do we need to do to an orange before we eat the inside part? What is the special skin called? Do we use the peel for anything? Invite the children to think about things they eat and drink that are lemon or orange flavoured (drinks, sweets, cakes, sauces, lollipops). What is the rhyme about? Explain that there is a special 'Oranges and lemons' ceremony held every year in March at Saint Clement Danes Church in London. It is a special service for children who are each given an orange and a lemon.

Follow-up activities

✧ Visit a supermarket and look at the different fruits available. Find out where they come from and how they are grown.

✧ Make a collection of fruit and sort them in different ways (does it have seeds, do you eat the outer skin, does it grow above the ground?).

✧ Set up an orange and lemon display and encourage the children to collect objects in these colours.

EGGS AND MORE EGGS

Objective

Design and Technology – To look at different ways of decorating eggs and design one using a range of materials.

Group size

Up to four children.

What you need

Six eggs, saucepan, water, edible food colour or fabric dyes, kitchen roll, vinegar, tablespoon, thin paintbrushes, sequins, ribbon, strong adhesive, glue spreaders, felt-tipped pens, assorted gummed shapes, tissue paper, vegetable oil, Plasticine, aprons, plastic cloth, scissors, basket, a selection of plastic containers.

Preparation

Hard boil the eggs and leave to cool. Dye the eggs different colours. If using fabric dyes, mix according to the instructions. Food colouring can be painted straight onto the eggs or diluted with water. Rub the eggs with tissue dipped in oil and leave overnight. (All this preparation to be carried out by an adult.)

Cover a table with a plastic cloth. Place the decorating materials in different plastic containers. Place dyed eggs in a basket. Put adhesive into a small container. Experiment with the different materials before doing this activity with the children to produce some decorated examples to encourage the children to make their own designs.

What to do

Gather the children round the table. Show the examples of decorated eggs. Explain that many years ago people decorated eggs to celebrate spring and the start of new life. Encourage the children to describe how the eggs have been decorated. Invite the children to design their own egg. Show them the different materials that are available and ask the children to think about how they could use the different materials.

Make sure the children are wearing aprons before they begin. Place small pieces of Plasticine on the table to secure the eggs while the children decorate them. Supervise the children if they ask you for help but encourage them to try their own designs. When the decorating is finished, place each egg in a safe place until dry. Gather the group together and invite the children to describe how they decorated their eggs. Leave the eggs on display in the basket until the children take them home. Make sure the children understand that the eggs must not be eaten.

Discussion

Are eggs usually these pretty colours? When do we give gifts of eggs to each other? Are they hens' eggs? Do you like to eat boiled eggs? What do you need to paint fine lines? How are you going to fasten the sequins (tissue paper, gummed shapes, ribbon) to the shell? Why can't we eat these eggs?

Follow-up activities

✧ Find out about other customs involving eggs (rolling eggs, Easter eggs, Easter egg hunt).
✧ Make a 'match the egg' game. Cut egg shapes out of card, decorate them with wrapping paper. Cut them into half in different ways and invite the children to match up the two halves.

CHAPTER 4
SPRING AROUND THE WORLD

The activities in this chapter will broaden children's knowledge and understanding of spring in other parts of the world. Traditions and festivals that are celebrated in different faiths at springtime are investigated.

TULIPS IN AMSTERDAM

Objective

PE – To develop movement through music.

Group size

Any size.

What you need

A tape recorder, tape of 'Tulips from Amsterdam', wall, table-top display space, map of Holland, pictures or posters of Dutch bulb fields, a vase of tulips, a tambour or tambourine, a large open space.

Preparation

Display the pictures or posters and the map. Place the vase of tulips on the display area. Gather the children together and show them the tulips. Point out and name the parts of the flower. Encourage the children to watch the buds unfold over the next few days. Explain that Holland is famous for tulips and many people visit the special fields where the flowers are grown.

What to do

Make sure the children are comfortably dressed or changed into loose clothing and wearing plimsolls or bare feet. Take them into the large space and ask them to sit and listen while you play the tape 'Tulips from Amsterdam'.

Ask them to each find a space and suggest that they imagine themselves to be tight tulip buds. Explain that when the tambour is played softly the 'buds' unfold making wide, outstretched petals. Repeat this several times. Suggest that the children show how the tulips would sway in the breeze in the fields.

Invite some of the children to be tulips and the others to be tulip gatherers. Encourage the children to imagine the tulip gatherers weaving in and out of the rows of tulips as they pick all the flowers. Play the music again and invite the children to make up their own movements.

Discussion

Explain that the tulip is one of the flowers we see in spring. Why do you think the Dutch people can grow lots of tulips? (Plenty of flat land and good soil.) What shapes, colours, sizes of tulips can we see? How does the music make you feel? Can you make up a tulip dance to go with the music?

Follow-up activities

✧ Visit a florist's shop or market stall to see the variety of tulips available.

✧ Find out more about Holland (dykes, windmills, food, flag, pottery, clogs, famous people, buildings).

SPRING IN AUSTRALIA

Objective

Geography – To find out about spring in a different country.

Group size

Any size.

What you need

A globe, a display board, paper, crayons, felt-tipped pens, scissors, adhesive, aprons. The book *Australia – Countries of the World* by Andrew Kelly (Wayland).

Preparation

Cover the display board and divide it up to show the calendar.

ARTWORK

Place the globe and pictures near the display. Prepare a table with the art materials.

What to do

Gather the children together near the display area. Point out the British Isles and Australia on the globe. Explain that the British Isles is in the Northern hemisphere and Australia is in the Southern hemisphere. Remind the children that the earth moves around the sun. Explain that when it is spring in the British Isles it is autumn in Australia, when it is autumn in the British Isles it is spring in Australia. Show the children the pictures in the book to reinforce the message.

Now suggest that the children make pictures of spring things in both countries to add to the display. These could include: flowers (primroses, daffodils), Christmas trees, a wattle tree, April showers, a maypole, crackers, swimming, a black swan.

Discussion

Why is the weather different in Australia? Where will the sun be shining when our days are cold? What is the special name for the northern part of the globe? What is the southern part of the globe called? What signs of spring do we see in this country? What signs of spring are seen in Australia? What do Australian people do in the spring?

Follow-up activities

✧ Mount an Australian exhibition showing pictures, artefacts, food and music.
✧ Make the role play area into an Australian beach café. Encourage the children to make 'play food' and write menus.
✧ Invite an Australian to come and talk to the children about spring in Australia.

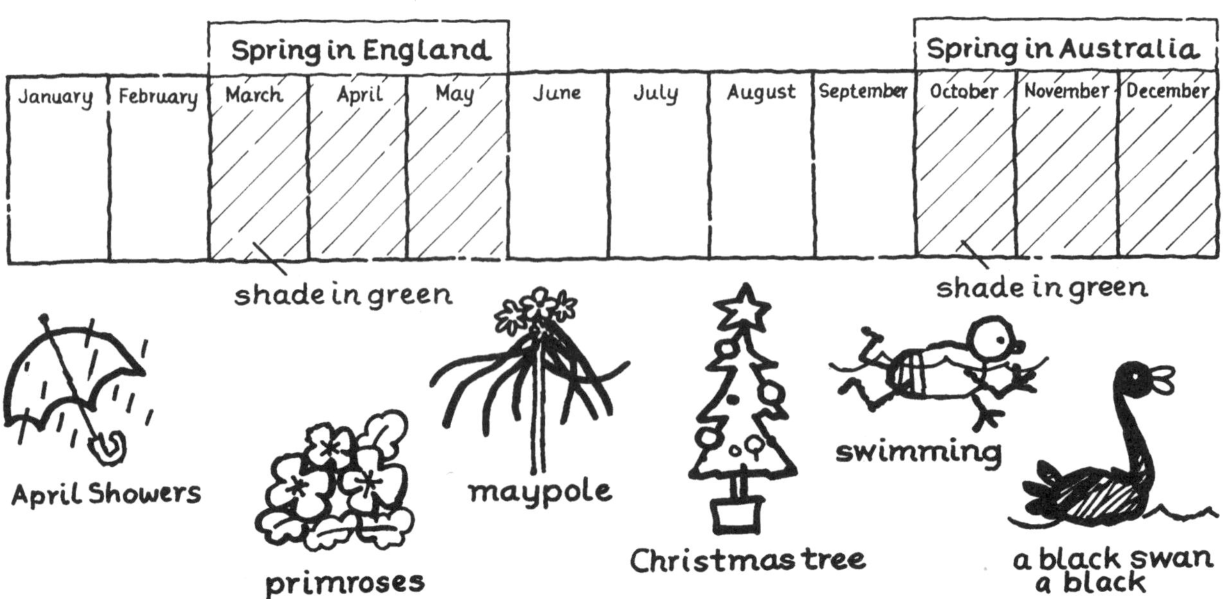

PENNSYLVANIA EGG TREE

Objective

Art – To create 2D mobiles, using different materials.

Group size

Six to eight children.

What you need

A multi-twigged branch, a large plant pot, sand, thick cardboard, scissors, newspaper or plastic cloth, aprons, strong adhesive, spreaders, poster or powder paints, brushes, a knife, cork, small waste cartons, carrot, potato, old magazines, different kinds of wrapping paper, a selection of buttons, sequin waste, plain and patterned coloured fabrics, needle and thread.

Preparation

Place the branch into the flower pot and secure with sand. Cut out different sizes of egg shapes from the thick card. Mix the paints thickly. Cut the potato into two and the carrot into about three chunks across the width, to make the vegetable stencils. Cut out sections of the potato to make patterns. Cut up the wrapping paper, magazines and fabrics into small squares or rectangles. Place the different art materials into plastic tubs. Cover and prepare the table and add the materials and equipment.

What to do

Show the children the 'potted' branch and explain that they are going to change this into a special 'egg tree'. Tell the children about the range of materials that will be available for use.

Invite the children to design their own eggs on the card shapes by printing or sticking on collage materials. Encourage them to think about how they are going to decorate them and which materials they could use. Suggest they try different materials. Give children support with sticking and printing if required.

When the eggs are complete, add a hanging loop using the needle and thread to each egg. Help the children to arrange their eggs on the tree.

Discussion

Ask the children how we celebrate Easter. Is Easter always in the season of spring? Ask children what kind of eggs they have. Explain that once long ago, people in Pennsylvania, America, made a special 'egg tree' to show how clever they were. They were poor people and had to use materials they already had. Why did they hang the eggs on the branch? How can we decorate our eggs? How can we get the eggs to hang on the tree?

Follow-up activities

✧ Find a large map of the USA and point out Pennsylvania.

✧ Talk about and try different ways of cooking eggs (scrambled, boiled, fried, poached). Carry out a survey to find the children's favourite.

✧ Make eggs using different media (papier mâché, flour and water dough, marzipan) and decorate them.

ST DAVID'S DAY

Objective

Geography – To learn about the principality and customs of Wales.

Group size

Large groups for introduction, groups of four for activity.

What you need

A large outline map of the United Kingdom, a Welsh flag, a daffodil, a leek, pictures of Welsh ladies in national costume, wooden 'dolly' pegs, tweed fabric, lace, black fabric, thin card, rubber bands, fine felt-tipped pens, strong adhesive, black coloured play dough.

Preparation

Select a suitable display area with wall and cupboard-top space. Shade the area of Wales on the map in red, green and white stripes and place this in the centre of the display wall. Arrange the pictures around it. Place the daffodil and leek on the cupboard top. Write labels saying 'Wales' and 'First of March is St David's Day' on the card. Secure these to the display. Make a Welsh peg dolly following the instructions below. Set up a separate craft table. Cut tweed fabric and lace into small rectangles and black fabric into triangles.

What to do

Show the children the Welsh display. Explain that the first of March is a very special day in Wales – St David's Day. Show the daffodil, leek and flag. Point out the ladies in Welsh costumes and show the children the peg doll dressed in national costume.

Organise the children into small groups and explain that they are each going to make a peg doll. Give each child a peg and ask them to use the fine felt-tipped pens to draw a face on the rounded end. Ask them to select a piece of tweed fabric, wrap this around the peg and secure it with an elastic band. Get the children to choose a lace 'apron', place it at the front of the doll and secure it under the elastic band. Attach the black 'shawls' round the upper part of the body and secure with a dab of adhesive. Make a Welsh hat from the black play dough and place this on the top of the peg.

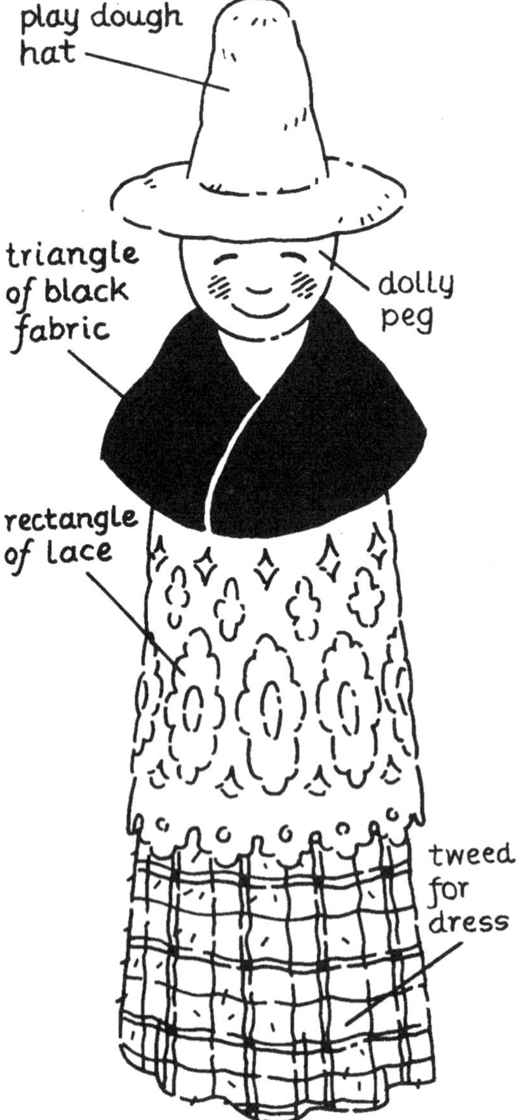

Discussion

Explain that St David is the special saint of Wales. Who are the saints for England, Ireland and Scotland? Why are the daffodil and leek special for Wales? Ask the children if they have visited Wales. Show the children the Welsh coastline. Do Welsh ladies wear their special costumes every day? When do we wear special clothes? Explain that Welsh people have a language of their own.

Follow-up activities

✧ Find out about and tell the story of St David in the *Book of Saints* (Ladybird).
✧ Collect pictures, postcards and souvenirs of 'Places in Wales' and add to the display.
✧ Find out about different Welsh food and make some Welsh cakes.

DOLLS' FESTIVAL

What to do

Gather the children around the display and draw their attention to the dolls. Ask each child in turn to describe their favourite doll and invite the other children to guess which doll is being described. Encourage the children to point out the differences between the dolls displayed to help identify them.

Point out Japan on the map and explain that dolls have their own special day in spring in that country. Japanese girls are given their own collection of beautiful dolls and on 3rd March all the dolls are set out on tiered shelves for everybody to enjoy.

Objective

English – To develop listening and thinking skills.

Group size

Any size.

What you need

A display area with a cupboard or table top, a collection of different dolls (baby, old, new, rag, foreign), some red and green fabric, building blocks or cardboard boxes, world map, pieces of white card, felt-tipped pens, crayons, drawing paper, a calendar showing the month of March.

Preparation

Hang the green fabric behind the display area to form a back drop. Pin up the calendar and map. Place the building blocks or boxes on the cupboard or table top and cover with the red fabric. Arrange the dolls and globe on the boxes. Write the captions 'Dolls' festival - 3rd March' and 'Can you find Japan?'. Place these on the display.

Discussion

Do we have a special day for dolls? What sort of dolls are there? What other special toys do you have? How could we have a special day for our toys? Shall we hold a special toy festival?

Follow-up activities

✧ Ask the children to bring in their favourite toys (with permission) and talk about them to the other children.
✧ Set up a Japanese display and include objects, music, pictures and posters.
✧ Find out about the Boys' festival in Japan. Get the children to make carp streamers and place them on bamboo canes.

HOLI – FESTIVAL OF COLOURS

Objective

RE – To develop an awareness of other religions and festivals.

Group size

Up to four children.

What you need

Holi by Olivia Bennett, The Way We Live series (Evans Bros) (or another book about the festival of Holi), brightly coloured card, adhesive, spreaders, orange and green lentils, dried rice, empty plastic containers, different coloured tubes of glitter, sequins, small beads, paper fastners, chalks, felt-tipped pens, newspaper, aprons.

Preparation

Cut the card into shapes (approximately 36cm × 18cm) to represent different types of doors (solid, with large or small window panes). Score a small rectangle (approximately 6cm × 4cm) to represent a letter box. Cut along three of the sides to make the flap. Cover a table with newspaper. Put lentils, rice, sequins, beads, paper fasteners and glitter into separate containers. Place aprons, cut-out doors, containers, felt-tipped pens, adhesive and spreaders on the table.

Tell the children about the Hindu festival of Holi. Explain that it is a special time for new life and the end of winter. Holi is a time for dancing and singing, and having fun. Families get ready for Holi by spring cleaning their homes and drawing special patterns (Rangoli) outside of their front doors. They use brightly coloured spices (turmeric and chilli), rice and sometimes powder paint and chalks.

What to do

Gather the children together on the carpet. Draw their attention to the materials and cut-out doors. Tell them they are going to make special patterns on the front doors to celebrate the coming of spring. Hold up a front door and ask the children what they have on their doors (letter box, number). Point out the different resources that can be used to make the patterns. Show the children how to make a trail using the glue and sprinkle some of the lentils and rice on to it.

Invite the children to make their own Rangoli patterns. Encourage them to design their own patterns that would celebrate the coming of spring. Help them to get different effects by experimenting with the glitter, chalks, felt-tipped pens and sequins. Remind them to put plenty of adhesive on the template so the materials are securely fastened. When the doors are finished, place on a flat surface and allow to dry. Get the children to add a door number and a door knob.

Discussion

How do Hindus celebrate this spring festival? Why do people make special patterns at fesitval times? (To welcome the gods and celebrate the coming of spring.) Discuss the way rangoli patterns are used to decorate the entrance to the houses. What happens to the glue when the patterns dry?

Follow-up activities

✧ Find and read stories of the Hindu gods Lord Krishna and Lord Shiva.
✧ Tell the children about the origins and tradition of April Fools' day.
✧ Learn the poem 'April fools' day' with the children.
✧ Read the poem 'Holi' on page 67.
✧ Collect a selection of information books to show different religious festivals at this time of year, for example Baisakhi (Sikh), Purim and Pesach (Jewish).

CHINESE DRAGONS

Objective

English – To develop understanding of the Chinese culture through a story.

Group size

Any size.

What you need

Thick coloured card, large and small sharp scissors, red, gold and orange tissue paper, gold and silver foil, garden sticks, strong adhesive, adhesive tape, felt-tipped pens, crayons, an old curtain, screen (easel or upturned cardboard box), a tape of Chinese music, ***China, the Culture*** by Bobbie Kalman (Crabtree Publishing Company) or another information book showing Chinese New Year Festival and Dragon parade.

Preparation

Cut a dragon shape (about 30cm) from the card. Cut scales from the coloured tissue. Ask the children to place these on one side of the dragon and stick them down. Cut out gold and silver scales and add these to give a shimmering effect. Place a garden stick at the head and rear of the undecorated side of the dragon. Secure the sticks with adhesive tape. Cut a template for the people and houses. Help the children to cut out people and houses from the thick card. Decorate these by colouring using felt-tipped pens (or any other materials available). Form the cut-out people into groups and fasten them together onto a stick and secure with adhesive tape. Do the same for the houses but attach these to the screen. Cut out a mountain peak and colour with crayons or felt-tipped pens. Secure the mountain peak to the edge of the screen. Place the 'theatre' so the children can see it easily. If making a screen, cover with the curtains. Place the finished 'stick puppets' on a table near the theatre.

What to do

Gather the children on the carpet near the 'puppet theatre'. Show them the information book pointing out the festivities for the Chinese New Year. Explain that Chinese New Year is a spring festival. Invite the children to watch the puppet show.

Put on the tape and tell the story:

A very old Chinese legend tells of a monster, a dragon, that ate people in China. The gods decided that the dragon must be kept inside a mountain to make sure people were safe. Once a year – during New Year – the dragon was allowed out. The Chinese kept him away from their houses by lighting fire crackers. The dragon was frightened away by the flashing and banging so the people were safe. Afterwards the dragon returned to his home in the mountain.

Encourage the children to make appropriate sounds as you speak to represent the fire crackers.

Explain that every year Spring is celebrated by the Chinese with parades of dragons and firecrackers.

Discussion

When do we celebrate New Year? Is it a spring celebration? Why do Chinese people have dragons in their parades? What special things do Chinese children do at this special time? (Have feasts, let off fire crackers, receive presents of money and stay up late.) How are the dragons' heads made? (Papier mâché.) Who is under the dragon's body to make the legs?

Follow-up activities

✧ Allow the children to retell the story using the puppets.
✧ Make a display showing Chinese food, music and other aspects of the culture.
✧ Learn the song 'Puff the magic dragon'.

ROGATIONTIDE

Objective

RE – To develop awareness of the countryside and the importance of spring for farmers.

Group size

Whole group.

What you need

A selection of vegetables, fruit, packets of seeds, garden flowers, grass and some toy animals (for example sheep, lambs). Pictures of farmers working on the land (showing harvesting, haymaking, tending animals), pieces of stiff card, scissors, adhesive, Plasticine.

Preparation

Collect the objects together. Cut out the farming pictures and mount on card. Form the Plasticine into thick sausages, insert the pictures so that they stand up. Cover a table with plain coloured fabric. Arrange the pictures and objects on the table.

What to do

Gather the children on the carpet around the table and show them the pictures and objects. Explain what each of the items are. Tell the children that there is a special spring service held in some churches on a day called Rogation Sunday. Explain that spring is an especially important time for farmers and other people who live and work in the countryside. Show the children the packets of seeds and tell them that farmers will be busy planting seeds in the fields so that there will be new crops in the summer and autumn seasons.

Encourage the children to think about the animals. Explain the different roles of the farmer during this time when new babies are born and need lots of attention. Select some of the vegetables and fruit and invite children to suggest how they are grown. Show some of the garden flowers and ask the children to think about the flowers that grow in gardens and parks in the summer months.

Invite children to focus on the objects on the table. Lead the children to think of this special service when Christians thank God for all these things and ask for his blessing on the seeds, fields, gardens and animals and all the people who work hard so that we have plenty of food to enjoy.

Discussion

During the discussion, try to draw out the similarities between ways of celebrating the coming of spring. Why do we plant things in the spring for later in the year? What weather will be best to help things grow? Are there places in the world where there isn't enough food to share? Help the children to realise that spring is a very special time and celebrations are carried out all over the world.

Follow-up activities

✧ Read and dramatise the Bible story of the parable of the sower, Matthew 13 verses 1-8.
✧ Visit the supermarket and investigate the fruit and vegetables from other countries.

CHAPTER 5 ANIMALS IN SPRING

As children begin to become aware of the world in which they live, it is important for them to appreciate the creatures that live in the environment. In this chapter we look at what happens to creatures in springtime.

ON THE FARM

Objective

Music – To learn a song involving sequences and animal sounds and sing it as part of a group.

Group size

Any size.

What you need

A copy of the song 'Old MacDonald had a farm', pictures of farm animals (sheep and lambs, sheep dogs, ducks and ducklings, pigs and piglets, cows and calves, hens, cocks and chicks, a cat), bamboo canes, thick card, adhesive tape, a large pair of scissors.

Preparation

Cut out the pictures of the farm animals. Sort into 'family' groups (adults and babies) and stick each group onto card. Cut around the animals in an irregular shape. Attach each shape to the top of the bamboo stick.

What to do

Show the children the animal canes and tell them what each group represents. Teach the song to the children asking them to join in with the animal sounds as you raise the appropriate cane. When they are familiar with the song introduce the idea of individual children holding the animal canes to prompt children with the sequence. Ask several children to stand up and make a line at the front of the group. Give each child an animal cane to hold.

Repeat the song encouraging the child to shout out the name of the animal they are holding, while the rest of the children remain quiet. Encourage all of them to sing the song, joining in with the animal sounds. Repeat the song several times allowing different children to take part.

Discussion

Ask the children the names of the animals and their babies. Explain that spring is a busy time on the farm as new babies are born. Have you seen new lambs in the fields? Where do baby chicks come from? What did we meet first on Old MacDonald's farm? Emphasise the need for the children to listen carefully to the words so they get the right sequence.

Follow-up activities

✧ Encourage children to think of other animals that might be on the farm (donkeys, owls, goats).
✧ Let the children sort the animals in a farmyard set. Encourage them to think where the animals might be in spring.
✧ Investigate different kinds of farms and find out what else happens during the spring (crops are sown, cows go out in the fields).
✧ Read the poem 'Visiting the farm' on page 68.

NEW LAMBS

Objective

Geography – To learn about the lambing season and the rearing of sheep.

Group size

Up to six children.

What you need

Pictures of different breeds of sheep, grey sugar paper, card or wooden lamb template, adhesive, glue spreaders, aprons, scissors, pencils, thick felt-tipped pen, thin card, balls of cream, black and brown knitting wool, blue and green frieze paper, an area of wall display, several cut-out ewes.

Preparation

If possible, arrange a visit to a farm to see new baby lambs, alternatively show the children some pictures of lambs and different breeds of sheep.

Prepare a frieze board using blue paper for the sky and cut green paper into shapes of hills. Draw and cut out several lamb and sheep templates. Cover a table with newspaper or a plastic cloth. Place other materials and equipment on the table.

What to do

Gather the children together and explain that spring is the time when the mother sheep has her new lambs. Tell them that the name for a mother sheep is a ewe, and that farmers often take the ewes into 'lambing sheds' to protect the new born lambs from any storms or cold weather.

Take the children to the table and suggest they make their own lambs using the materials provided. Show them how to draw round the sheep templates and help each child to cut out a sheep. Encourage the children to use the different coloured wools to decorate their sheep. Allow the children to work in pairs or individually to make some ewes. Ask the children to add their sheep to the frieze. Add

the caption 'Spring lambs are born on the farm'.

Discussion

Ask the children why they think it is better for lambs to be born in the spring. Why does the farmer take the ewes into a 'lambing shed'? How many lambs does the ewe usually have? If they have seen lambs playing, encourage them to describe what the lambs were doing. What do the lambs feed on? Do all sheep look the same? Point out the different colours and breeds. Why do farmers keep sheep?

Follow-up activities

✧ Tell the Bible story of the lost sheep, Luke 15, verses 3-6 or Matthew 18, verses 12-13.
✧ Make a list of all the different things we use that are made of wool. Start a collection and invite the children to add their own objects.
✧ Set up a 'lambing time' for the model farm. Encourage the children to make lambing sheds using junk boxes and lambs from Plasticine.
✧ Read the poem 'It must be Springtime' on page 70.

WAKING UP

Objective

PE/Drama – To use movement to represent different creatures.

Group size

Whole group.

What you need

Large pictures or drawings of a hedgehog, a dormouse, a ladybird, a frog, a grass snake, a bumble bee, a tortoise and a butterfly. Thick card, scissors, adhesive, thick felt-tipped pen, adhesive film, a large open space, two chime bars, beater.

Preparation

Mount the pictures onto thick card. Write the names of each creature on the back of the relevant picture card. Cover with adhesive film.

Tell the children that animals (hedgehogs, dormice, frogs, ladybirds) who have been asleep (hibernating) during the winter, start to wake up in the spring.

What to do

Gather all the children into the large space and show them the pictures of the creatures. Encourage them to name the creatures and describe what movements they might make when they wake up in the spring.

Ask the children to crouch or lay in a sleeping position on the floor. Play the chime bars to create a tick-tock sound, telling the children to listen carefully. Tap one of the chime bars fast to represent an alarm clock and say 'Wake up, wake up, you sleepy head, Spring is here so come out of your bed!'.

Choose a creature card, hold it up and ask one of the children to identify the creature. Invite the children to show how that creature might wake up and move about in spring. Repeat several times with the other creatures, inviting the children to demonstrate their movements.

Discussion

Discuss how the different creatures might wake up (stretching, yawning, wriggling, moving slowly, quickly). Why do the creatures wake up in spring? Encourage the children to think about the places the creatures would be when they awake (frog - in the pond, hedgehog - in a pile of leaves, tortoise – in a cardboard box filled with straw). How would they feel? (Hungry, thirsty, lively, sleepy.)

Follow-up activities

✧ Find out about and make a list of creatures that hibernate and those that do not. Collect pictures of creatures that do not hibernate and mount these on card. Add to the cards of creatures that do hibernate. Encourage the children to sort and classify according to different criteria (those that can fly, have four legs, hibernate, lay eggs).

✧ Make zigzag books to show the sequence of the seasons and the habits of the creatures.

✧ Read the story 'Wake up – it's spring' on page 81.

CUCKOO, CUCKOO

Objective

PE/Drama – To develop awareness of space and play a simple game.

Group size

Any size.

What you need

A large open space, four or five large plastic hoops, a large ball.

Preparation

Tell the children about the cuckoo, explaining that it arrives in Britain from Africa in April and is recognised by its special call. Tell them that it is a lazy bird as it doesn't build its own nest, but lays its eggs in nests of other birds. Collect the hoops and ball ready for the game. Make sure the children are comfortably dressed or changed into loose clothing and wearing plimsolls or bare feet.

What to do

As a warm-up activity, ask the children to move around the large space using different movements (walking, skipping, running, hopping). Introduce the idea of stopping and starting to the cuckoo call.

Gather the children together and tell them they are going to play the 'Cuckoo called' game. Give the hoops out to some of the children and ask them to place the hoops in spaces around the room (make sure these are evenly spaced).

Explain that they are going to move around the space without touching the hoops or each other. The sound of the cuckoo ('Cuckoo, cuckoo') will give the signal to start moving. Stand in the centre of the space and choose one of the children to be the cuckoo and hold the ball (cuckoo's egg). When you shout 'Cuckoo's coming', all the children must move to stand inside any of the hoops. The child with the ball goes to one of the hoops, stands inside and gives one of the other children the ball. The child with the ball comes to the centre and the game is repeated.

Discussion

In what season does the cuckoo return? How do we recognise the cuckoo's call? Why is the cuckoo called a lazy bird? Where does it lay its eggs? Ask the children to reflect on how the other birds feel when the cuckoo lays its eggs in their nest. Does the cuckoo stay and look after her babies? Explain that the cuckoo baby is often bigger than the other baby birds and takes their food. It often pushes the other baby birds out of the nest to make more room for itself.

Follow-up activities

✧ Listen to a tape of the cuckoo's call. Find out more about the cuckoo. What happens to its call later in the year? Where does it go to in the summer?
✧ Read the poem 'Winter to Spring' on page 71, invite the children to join in with the 'Cuckoo'.
✧ Learn the poem 'The new nest' with the children.

SPOT THE LADYBIRD

Objective

Mathematics – To develop counting and early addition.

Group size

Four to six children

What you need

Photocopiable sheet on page 93, scissors, number line showing numbers 1 to 7, large dice with spots, black and red felt-tipped pens, poster paints or crayons, adhesive plastic film, thick card, thin black card.

Preparation

Make photocopies of the activity sheet so that each child has two ladybirds. Colour the ladybirds but don't add any spots. Mount the ladybirds onto separate pieces of thick card and cover with adhesive plastic film. Cut out spots from the black card sufficient for each ladybird. Place the spots in a box lid. Place all the objects on a table.

What to do

Gather the children round a table and show them the ladybirds. Encourage the children to identify what is missing from the ladybirds.

Explain that you have a game called 'Spot the ladybird' where the ladybirds can get back their spots. The children need to throw the dice and count the number of spots (with support if necessary). They then collect this number of spots for their ladybird and place them on one side of the wing. Each ladybird must have seven spots all together to finish the

game. Encourage the children to take turns to throw the dice.

When some spots have been added ask them to count how many more are needed to make seven. When the children have their next turn they can try and complete a ladybird or start to 'spot' the next one. The winner is the child who correctly completes the two ladybirds by throwing the exact number to finish.

Discussion

How do we recognise a ladybird? What colours are they? (The best known ladybird is red and has seven black spots although they can come in all sorts of colours.) What happens to ladybirds in the spring? (They wake up after their winter sleep, and baby ladybirds are hatched.) Where do you see ladybirds? Explain that ladybirds are good friends to the gardener as they eat lots of greenflies. What does the dice say? How many spots can you collect? How many more spots do you need?

Follow-up activities

- Read the information book *The Ladybird* First Discovery series (Moonlight Publishing).
- Learn the rhyme 'Ladybird, ladybird, fly away home'.
- Make large ladybirds from paper bags and collage materials.

FLYING BACK

Objective

Geography – To develop awareness of different parts of the world through the migration of birds.

Group size

Up to four children.

What you need

A large basic map of the world, pictures of different kinds of birds (swallows, swifts, cuckoos, martins), bird templates, thin coloured card, coloured tissue paper, adhesive, glue spreaders, thin white paper, crayons, a darning needle, strong thread, large pair of scissors, pencils, short garden sticks, the rhyme 'Two little dicky birds'.

Preparation

Teach the children the rhyme 'Two little dicky birds'. Secure the world map and bird pictures to an easel or blackboard. Place craft materials on a table.

What to do

Gather the children together and say the rhyme 'Two little dicky birds'. Show the children the map and point out some of the countries that the birds go to (North Africa, Asia and Europe). Name the well known birds that migrate (swallows, cuckoo, house martins, spotted flycatcher, turtle dove).

Invite the children to make some birds. Show them the materials on the prepared table and demonstrate how to draw round the bird template and then cut a short slit in the middle of the body.

Next, show the children how to take a strip of white paper and fold it like a concertina. Push the folded paper through the slit and pull out the concertina folds to form the wings. Suggest the children colour the paper before folding it to make brightly coloured wings for their own birds.

When the birds are finished, thread thick cotton through the top of the body and attach them to garden sticks.

Discussion

Explain that some birds fly away to warmer countries when the weather gets cold. When spring comes the birds fly back, to spend the warmer months here. Where do the birds go? How do they get to other countries? Introduce and explain the words 'migrate', 'flocks', 'formation' and 'flight paths'. Ask the children which birds can be seen in our country throughout the year.

Follow-up activities

✧ Set up a bird table with regular food and record the number and frequency of birds who visit.
✧ Listen to the 'dawn chorus' on a tape of bird song.
✧ Find out what kinds of birds live in hot countries all through the year.

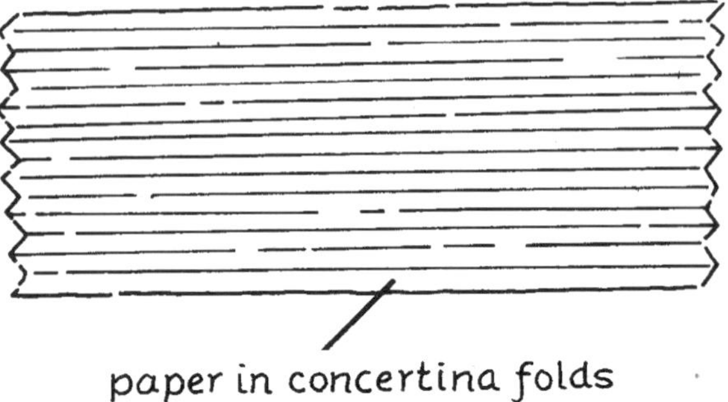

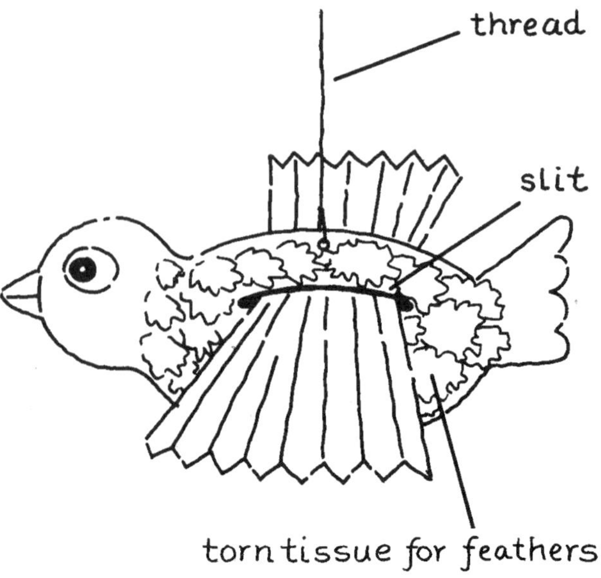

MARCH HARE

Objective

Art – To learn about the work of a famous artist.

Group size

Up to six children.

What you need

A reproduction of Albrecht Dürer's drawing of the hare (widely available on postcards in stationery shops or art books). Large sheets of thick white paper, newspaper or plastic cloth, aprons, pieces of charcoal, soft lead pencils, sheets of coloured card, staples and stapler, an easel or board.

Preparation

Display the reproduction of Dürer's hare on the easel or board. Cover the table. Put out an apron and drawing materials for each child. Make 'picture frames' out of the coloured card. Use information books to find out about hares and point out the differences between hares and rabbits.

What to do

Gather the children on the carpet and show them the picture of the hare. Explain that it is a famous drawing by an artist called Dürer who lived in Germany hundreds of years ago and liked to paint and draw things from nature. Point out the shape of the hare's body, the ears, whiskers and feet. Encourage the children to describe how Dürer drew the fur to make it look real.

Invite the children to create their own March hare drawings. Display the Dürer reproduction and other pictures of hares in the information books while the children work. Before they begin their drawings ask them to think which drawing materials they would like to use. Move around the group and offer encouragement as they draw.

When they have finished work, get them to sign their drawings and then choose a frame

for their work. Secure the frames with staples. Display the children's work alongside the Dürer picture.

Discussion

What is the difference between a hare and a rabbit? (Hares are usually seen alone, rabbits in groups, hares are larger with longer ears and hind legs, baby hares or leverets are able to hop almost after birth.) Explain that the hare is called the 'mad March hare' because it runs and leaps about in March. Male hares (jacks) stand on their back legs and appear to be 'kicking' and 'boxing'. How did Dürer make his hare's fur look real? Does it seem as though the hare's eye is looking at us? Why do artists sign their names on their work?

Follow-up activities

✧ Read the poem 'Mad March hare' on page 70.

✧ Collect stories, poems and rhymes about hares and rabbits (for example, ***Alice in Wonderland, The Hare and the Tortoise***).

✧ Find out about other 'animal paintings' by well-known artists. Collect some postcard reproductions and make them into an art album.

✧ Ask if any child has a pet rabbit and invite them to bring it in (under supervision).

BUSY BEES

Objective

Music – To develop awareness of sound and rhythm.

Group size

Whole group.

What you need

A cassette of ***The Flight of the Bumble Bee*** by Rimsky-Korsakov, an information book about bees and wasps, combs, tracing paper, empty washing-up liquid bottles, rice, dried peas, pasta, adhesive tape, cheese graters, wooden spoons, metal bottle tops, strong wire, string, a large basket or box.

Preparation

Wash and sterilise the combs and cover with tracing paper. Place dried peas, rice or pasta separately into the empty washing-up liquid bottles and secure the tops with adhesive tape. Place instruments in the basket or box. Listen to the cassette and use the cassette counter to identify the parts of the music on which you want to focus.

What to do

Gather the group together and read the information book about bees and wasps to the children. Show them the pictures and use them for discussion. Play a section from ***The Flight of the Bumble Bee.*** Ask the children to listen carefully.

Show the children the home-made percussion instruments and suggest that they find out which of them sound most like bees. Allow the children to experiment and then demonstrate the sounds they have found. Play the cassette again and invite the children to add their bumble bee sounds as an accompaniment.

Discussion

Tell the children that the queen bee is very important. She wakes up from hibernation and starts to search for a new nest. What do bees feed on? (The early spring flowers.) What sounds do the bees make? What does the bee make that is sweet and sticky? (Honey.) Encourage the children to listen to the music and imagine the bee flying around. Can we make bee sounds with our instruments? Which instruments make the best sounds for bees? Can you hear a rhythm in the music? (Buzz, buzz, buzzy bee.) Invite the children to copy the rhythm.

Follow-up activities

✧ Read the poem 'Brown bees' by Irene F Pawsey from ***A Book of a Thousand Poems*** (Evans).
✧ Make giant bees and a beehive.
✧ Show the children different types of honey and a honeycomb.
✧ Use the photocopiable sheet 'Buzz off!' on page 94.

CHAPTER 6 NEW BEGINNINGS

Spring can be a chance for new beginnings and change. Activities in this chapter take a look at spring weddings, spring cleaning and changes in the animal world.

WEDDING BELLS

Objective

English – To write a group story.

Group size

Six to eight children.

What you need

A quiet area, the book ***When Willie Went to the Wedding*** by Judith Kerr (Fontana). A collection of photographs showing different kinds of weddings (church, mosque, temple, register office). An easel or board, large sheet of pale coloured paper, thick felt-tipped pen.

Preparation

Place the easel in a prominent position and attach the paper to it. Place the story book and wedding photographs nearby.

What to do

Show the wedding photographs to the children and explain that people often choose to get married in spring. Encourage the children to discuss differences in the wedding clothes and notice the different settings for the weddings.

Read the book, ***When Willie Went to the Wedding***, which is a story about a little boy who takes his pets to a wedding and describes the fun that this causes. Discuss the main points of the story. Invite the children to write their own group story with an unusual animal turning up at the wedding and doing funny things. Encourage the children to think about how the story should start.

Gather the children's ideas and discuss them. Ask the children to decide on the characters, animal and incidents at the wedding. Act as scribe, writing down the group's ideas on the large sheets of paper until you have a group story.

Discussion

Have you ever been to a wedding? Where was it held? Why do people choose to get married in spring? Where are the different places people can get married? Why do people wear special clothes at a wedding? What did Willie think would happen to his animals at the wedding? How does the story start? What could happen next? How does the story end?

Follow-up activities

✧ Set up the role play area so the children can organise different kinds of weddings.
✧ Make a display of weddings from different cultures. Ask people to come and talk about wedding celebrations.
✧ Organise a visit to a building where weddings are held (mosque, register office, church, temple).

IDEAL HOME

Objective

Design and Technology – To design and make a model nursery.

Group size

Four to six children.

What you need

A baby catalogue, a large cardboard box, a selection of old wallpaper, different fabrics (plain, patterned, textures), waste boxes (different sizes and shapes), rubber bands, empty cotton reels, plastic tops, scissors, white paper, felt-tipped pens, wallpaper paste, small paint and paste brushes, strong adhesive, spreaders, poster paints, play dough, Plasticine, paper fasteners, plastic cloth, aprons, two activity tables.

Preparation

Place the large box onto a table with the open side at the top. Make two vertical cuts down the front facing side to make a 'pull down' front. Prepare the activity tables. Assemble all the materials and tools and place on one of the tables. This gives the children opportunity to look at and select the displayed materials and tools, It also encourages children to work in 'uncluttered' space. Place the prepared box in a prominent place.

What to do

Set the scene by asking the children to describe what happens when a new baby arrives in the family. Invite them to relate their own experiences of preparing for a new baby, describing the clothes and equipment a new baby needs. Show them the baby catalogue and point out some of the items.

Suggest that the children design and make a model of a nursery for a new baby. Show them the prepared box and encourage them to think about decorating it to make a baby's room. Ask them to think about what furniture would be suitable.

Allow the children to work in pairs or individually, using the boxes and materials available. Explain that the furniture needs to fit inside the 'model room'. Support the children in carrying out their ideas and encourage them to find ways of simplifying/improving their ideas.

When they have finished, allow the furniture and 'room' to dry thoroughly. Invite the children to add their models and reflect on their design.

Discussion

What does a new baby need? (Cot, bath, chest of drawers, toy box, mobile, lamp, curtains, carpet.) How could we decorate the walls? What colours shall we use? How shall we make the cot? Would there be a window? How can we fasten the curtains? How is wallpaper put on? In small pieces or long strips? Would this make a good nursery for a baby?

Follow-up activities

- Read 'The very first story' from ***My Naughty Little Sister*** by Dorothy Edwards (Methuen).
- Invite a mum with a new baby in to talk to the children. Ask her to bring in and talk about some of the equipment and clothes the new baby needs.
- Set up the role play area as a nursery.

SPRING CLEANING

Objective

PE/Drama – To model some cleaning activities and create a story in mime.

Group size

Large group or class.

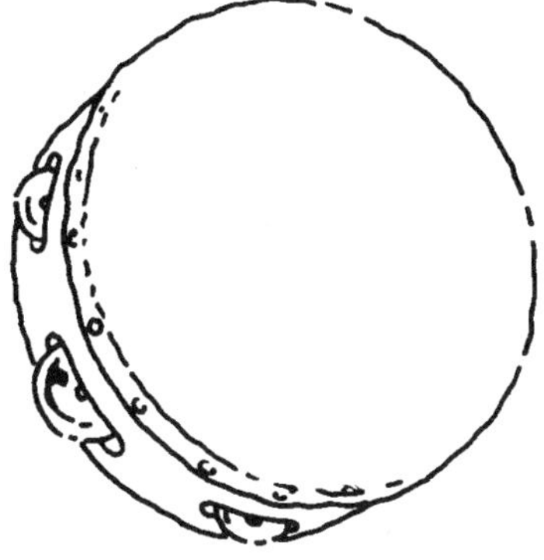

What you need

A small tambourine or tambour, a large space.

Preparation

Talk to the children about how they would spring clean their bedrooms. Discuss what they would have to clear and how they would clean. Suggest cleaning tools and materials.

What to do

Take the children to the large space and ask them to work in pairs. Encourage each pair to find a space of their own to represent their 'room'. Start by asking the children to mime picking everything from the floor. What would you pick up and where would you put things? (Toys into boxes, books onto bookcases, clothes onto hangers or folded into drawers.) Beat a steady rhythm on the instrument as children mime these actions, bending down low and then stretching up high. Suggest, 'Now make the bed together. Smooth the sheet, shake the pillow and smooth the duvet or cover.' Beat a slightly different rhythm for each, for example daa-de-dum for smooth the sheet, dum-diddy-diddy for shake the pillows.

Ask the children what we do next? Would it be vacuuming the floor? Get one child to mime moving furniture while the other plugs in, switches on and uses the vacuum cleaner. Next comes the dusting. Each child pretends to take a duster and dusts the room to a soft, steady beat. Finally window cleaning. Each child takes a section of window and sprays it, then polishes it, rubbing hard to give a gleam. Beat a lively, slightly frenzied, 'polishing' rhythm. Say, 'Now the room is spotlessly clean. You are very tired. Creep slowly and quietly to bed and go straight to sleep.'

Discussion

Talk about the custom of 'spring cleaning' after the winter. If you 'spring cleaned' your bedroom what would you do first? What would you do to clean the floor? How would you clean the tops of cupboards and shelves? What would you use to clean the windows? What might happen if we don't clean our rooms?

Follow-up activities

✧ Find out about spring cleaning customs and festivals in other countries (for example, before Holi and the Jewish Passover, the Japanese festival of 'Setsubun').
✧ Teach the children the action rhyme 'Spring cleaning' on page 72.
✧ Organise a 'spring turnout' and sort, recycle or throw out objects. Donate useful items to charity (hospitals, organisations for developing countries).
✧ Learn the song 'Spring cleaning' on page 79.
✧ Read the story 'Daisy's spring clean' on page 88.

BUILDING TIME

Objective

Technology – To make edible nests using different ingredients.

Group size

Up to four children.

What you need

Ingredients: 50g of soft margarine, two 15ml spoons of golden syrup, 50g of drinking chocolate (sifted), 25g of cornflakes, 25g of bran cereal, a packet of mini eggs (makes 16 nests.)

Equipment: aprons, a cooker or ring, pair of metric scales, a measuring spoon, 16 paper cake cases, a pan, a wooden spoon, two large plastic bowls, two large metal spoons, four teaspoons, baking sheet, small tins or plastic containers (for each child to take 'nests' home). Large piece of coloured card, a felt-tipped pen.

Preparation

Cover and prepare the table for the activity.

What to do

Make sure each child puts on an apron and washes his/her hands. Gather the children round the table. Measure out the margarine and golden syrup into the pan and place on a low heat until they have melted. Remove from the heat. Measure the drinking chocolate and ask a child to stir it in.

Pour the mixture into the two bowls. Measure the cornflakes and encourage the children to stir until the cornflakes are thoroughly coated with the chocolate mixture. Repeat this process with the bran cereal.

Suggest another child sets out the paper cases on the baking sheet. Give each child a spoon and invite the children to choose a mixture to make their nests, then spoon it into the baking cases. Ask each child to press down the middle of the 'nest', choose some mini eggs and place them inside. Leave to cool. When set allow each child to put their nests in a container to take home.

Discussion

Explain that birds are very busy building their nests in spring. Encourage the children to think of materials that birds use for building (twigs, sticks, moss, sheep's wool, feathers). What ingredients are used to make the edible nests? How do we make sure we have the correct amount? Why do the cornflakes and bran cereal need to be coated with the chocolate mixture? (So that the mixture sticks together.) How many eggs will fit in? How many nests will each child have to take home?

Follow-up activities

✧ Give the children a copy of photocopiable page 95, the activity sheet 'Building time'. Talk about each picture and relate it to the birds building nests to lay their eggs. Ask the children to cut out the pictures and place them on to another sheet of paper to show the correct sequence; stick in place when an adult has checked the order.

✧ Find out about the different nests birds build and the different locations they are found.

EGGS TO CHICKS

Objective

English – To develop different writing styles through observation and recording.

Group size

Any size.

What you need

An incubator, nearby electrical socket, eight suitable eggs, jug, water, a flip chart, an easel, paper, felt-tipped pen.

Preparation

Organise the loan of an incubator from a farm or a nature or teachers' centre. Ask for instructions about what to do with the eggs and what to expect to see during the incubation period. Set up the incubator in a suitable place in your room. Number the eggs 1 to 8 using the felt-tipped pen. Place the eggs in the incubator according to the recommendations of the farmer, nature or teachers' centre. Make sure that the plug is placed firmly in the socket. Make a label 'Do not turn off at any time'. Set up the flip chart on the easel.

What to do

Gather the children around the incubator. Point out to the group that this is a special piece of equipment which uses electricity to keep the eggs warm. Explain that it is similar to the mother hen sitting on the eggs. It is important to keep the eggs moist and to turn them over each day. Tell the children that they will need to look at the eggs every day and write down any changes.

Gather the children around the flip chart. Invite them to record their observations as a diary to show what has happened to the eggs. Write the day and date on the first page of the flip chart. Encourage the children to suggest the wording for each day's entry while you act as scribe to record their observations. Read aloud the previous days' entry before writing the next. Invite children to illustrate the diary entry or take photographs. Each week make time to read through the week's diary.

Make sure that chick food and water are available for the chicks when they start to hatch. You will need to find suitable homes for the chicks, too.

Discussion

Where do chickens come from? Who lays eggs? Discuss the role of the incubator and how it works. Why do we need an incubator? What will happen to the eggs? How can we describe what has happened to the egg? Explain that the diary gives a record of what has happened day by day. How does the chicken get out of the egg? What does it look like? Is it fluffy? Does it look like a hen?

Follow-up activities

✧ Make a hatching chicken by placing yellow pompom chicks inside an empty eggshell.
✧ Find out what other animals lay eggs (dinosaurs, frogs, snakes).
✧ Make a collection of poems, rhymes and stories about eggs, hens and chickens.
✧ Read the poem 'The gosling song' on page 69.

TADPOLES TO FROGS

Objective

Science – To develop understanding of the life cycle of the frog.

Group size

Up to four children.

What you need

Thick white and blue card, strong adhesive, glue stick, scissors, adhesive film, felt-tipped pens, information book showing pictures of the life cycle of a frog.

Preparation

Draw the different stages of the frog (a blob of jelly with a black dot, blobs of jelly with a tail developing, tadpole with tail, tadpole with front legs developing, tadpole with back legs developing and a frog) onto an A4 sheet of white paper. Make eight photocopies. Stick four of the photocopies onto the thick white card and cover with adhesive film, then cut the page into six sections. Use the blue card to cut four pond shapes. Take the remaining photocopies and cut these into sections. Stick a set of pictures onto each pond. Cover them with adhesive film.

What to do

Place the 'ponds' and cards on a table. Ask the children to sit around the table and show them the 'ponds'. Look at the pictures and encourage the children to describe what the pictures represent. Show the children the separate matching cards. Shuffle them and place them in the middle of the table. Give each child a pond.

To play the game, let each child in turn take a card from the middle of the table and match it with a picture on their pond. The children continue to match the pictures until someone completes the life cycle of the frog. If a child takes the same card, it is returned to the bottom of the pile.

Discussion

What happens to frogs in the spring? (They come out of hibernation, return to the pond and lay eggs.) Do frogs have baby frogs? Does frogspawn float or sink? What is the jelly around the black dot? Which part of the tadpole grows first? What happens to the jelly around the tadpole? Explain that the back legs develop before the front legs until finally the frog appears. What other creatures lay eggs? Why does a frog need strong back legs?

Follow-up activities

- Sing the rhyme 'Five little speckled frogs' and invite the children to dramatise it.
- Keep a frog log of frogspawn/tadpoles changing into frogs.
- Make frog puppets (finger, stick and paper bag).
- Learn the song 'I'm a frog' on page 75.

CATERPILLAR DETECTIVES

Objective

Mathematics – To develop understanding of size, sequence and exchanging.

Group size

Up to four children.

What you need

Thick green, yellow, brown, red, blue and purple card, A5 paper, gummed shapes, a 10p coin, small jar lid, green felt or other material, adhesive, scissors, felt-tipped pens, a dice, white gummed label, a shaker.

Preparation

Leaves (baseboards) – cut four large leaves out of the thick card. Use as template and cover with material. Cut around leaf shapes. Carefully stick the material onto card.

Eggs (×4) – draw round the coin, move the coin along, and draw round again. Keep doing this until you have formed a cluster of about six 'eggs'. Draw round the outline with a felt-tipped pen and cut out.

Caterpillars (×4) – take the jar lid and draw five overlapping circles on the green card. Cut out and draw segments, hairs, eyes, mouth and feelers.

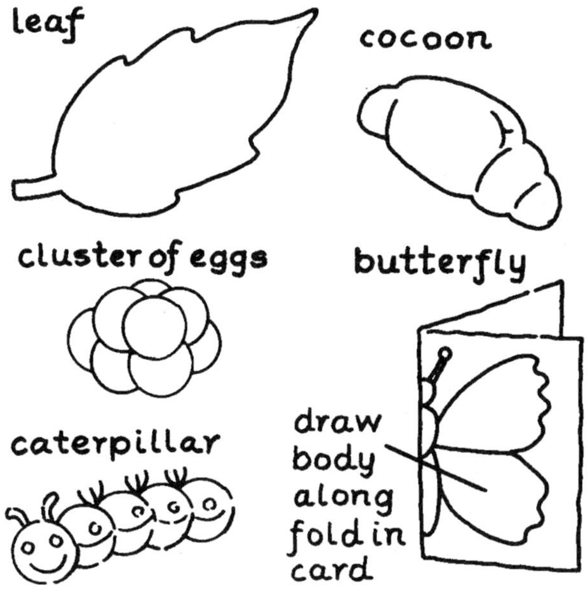

Cocoon (×4) – draw a cocoon shape on the brown card and cut out.

Butterflies (×4) – fold the A5 paper in half. Draw the outline of a butterfly. Cut out and use this template on the coloured card. Add features and stick on gummed shapes to form symmetrical patterns.

Draw small pictures of eggs, a caterpillar, cocoon and butterfly on the gummed paper. Cut into small sections and stick a picture onto four sides of the dice.

What to do

Gather the children together and introduce the caterpillar game. Show the different parts and explain the life cycle of the butterfly: the butterfly lays a cluster of eggs on a leaf, out of the eggs come little caterpillars, the caterpillar eats and eats, it grows larger and larger until it turns into a hard cocoon. The cocoon splits and out comes a butterfly.

Give each child a leaf. Show the children the dice and identify the pictures. Explain that the object of the game is to follow the life cycle of the butterfly, and the objects have to be collected in sequence. Ask a child to throw the dice. If the picture shows eggs, the child collects them and puts them on his leaf. When a caterpillar is thrown, the eggs can be exchanged for the caterpillar.

Discussion

Where do we find caterpillars? What do they look like? Explain that caterpillars can make our skin itch and we should not touch them. Do you know what is inside the cocoon? Why does it have a hard shell? When do we see butterflies and moths? What is special about the patterns on the wings?

Follow-up activities

✧ Teach the children the action rhyme 'Butterfly inside' on page 69.
✧ Set up an observation tank so that children can watch caterpillars over a short period.
✧ Learn the song 'I went to the cabbages one day' from *Tinderbox* (A & C Black).
✧ Dramatise the story of *The Hungry Caterpillar* by Eric Carle (Picture Puffin).

A SPECIAL BIRTHDAY

Objective

History – To learn about a famous person from the past.

Group size

Any size.

What you need

The Ugly Duckling by Hans Christian Anderson (Ladybird), a blank birthday card, a calendar for the month of April, an old shoe, a tambourine, a top hat, a puppet.

Preparation

Read the story *The Ugly Duckling.* Circle 2 April on the calendar. Place all the objects on the table except the birthday card.

What to do

Gather the children on the carpet. Show them *The Ugly Duckling* book and remind them of the story. Explain that the story was written a long time ago by a famous man, called Hans Christian Anderson, who lived in Denmark. Show the calendar and ask the children which date is marked. Tell the children that Hans Christian Anderson was born on 2 April and it is his special day.

Explain that Hans' father was a cobbler (show the shoe) but when he died Hans had to leave school to help his mother. He loved reading and making toy theatres and puppets (show puppet), but he really wanted to be a singer. He left home and went to see a famous dancer. He put on his top hat and played his tambourine (show objects) but the dancer just laughed and said he was terrible. So instead he started writing fairy stories. *The Ugly Duckling* was the most famous.

Suggest that together you can celebrate Hans' birthday. Show the children the card and invite them to give a message. Scribe the message and show the children the card. Place it on the display. Invite the children to look at the objects and read the story.

Discussion

Explain that *The Ugly Duckling* is a fairy story. Some stories are real and some made up. Hans Christian Anderson used the story of the ugly duckling to show how people could hurt each other by unkind words and actions. What is the name given to people who write books? Why do we celebrate people's birthdays? Why was Hans upset by the dancer? What did he decide to do? Invite the children to find other stories written by Hans Christian Anderson.

Follow-up activities

✧ Hold a favourite book day and encourage children to share their stories.
✧ Ask an author to visit and talk about how he/she gets ideas for his/her books.
✧ Encourage children to write their own stories and make them into a book.
✧ Familiarise children with the vocabulary of books (page, illustration, author, words, index).

CHAPTER 7 DISPLAYS

Displays provide an opportunity to reflect the children's completed work and also to stimulate further learning. They do not need to be static but can be changed and added to regularly.

CREATING A DISPLAY

Develop short- and long-term displays using a range of surfaces, for example walls, table tops and cupboards. Include both 2D and 3D presentations to make your displays more effective. Displays should reflect not only the work children have done but can also be used to stimulate further learning. Use a variety of areas throughout the building to stimulate discussion and to inform other people about the work that is being undertaken.

Involve the children in creating the displays, ensuring that both adults' and children's work is presented. Displays should be interactive - designed to enable children to participate whenever possible. Children should be able to see and handle displays and be encouraged to engage with the objects included as much as possible.

Captions on all displays are very important, with the lettering bold and clearly written or created using a word processor. Involve the children in producing the captions, as opportunities to use information technology can develop the children's keyboard and writing skills. The results will be eye-catching captions and labels produced using different fonts and sizes of text, ready for your displays.

Basics of display

Use a wide selection of materials for backing displays. Include frieze paper, rolls of wallpaper, hessian, lengths of fabric, polystyrene tiles, brightly coloured card and sugar paper.

Position boxes, packaging and containers of different shapes and sizes to give height and depth to a table or cupboard-top display and to add an effective three-dimensional element to a standard wall display.

Complement your basic display materials with wallpaper borders, gift paper, pieces of garden trellis, rolls of sequin waste, pieces of fabric, ribbon, string, net, natural objects (dried flowers, stones, pebbles, pieces of wood), waste materials, tulle, felt and corrugated card. Label and store the materials accessibly.

SPRING CELEBRATIONS

What you need

Portable screens or display boards, backing paper, two small tables, scissors. Fabric to cover the tables, staples, stapler, coloured thin and thick card, thick felt-tipped pens, crayons, paper, poster or powder paints, brushes, a calendar. Pictures, photographs, posters and children's paintings and collages of festivals celebrating spring such as Holi (festival of colours), St David's Day, May Day, Pancake Day and Chinese New Year. Cards (bought and made by the children) for birthday, Mothering Sunday, Holi, Easter and Chinese New Year. Frying pan, eggs, butter, milk, flour, whisk, wooden spoon and a selection of toppings for pancakes. A leek, a Welsh peg doll, a map of Wales and other Welsh artefacts. Examples of stories written by Hans Christian Anderson, pictures of ducklings, cygnets, swans and ducks. Information and fictional books related to spring festivals and celebrations.

This is an interactive display which relates to activities in Chapter 3, 4 and 6. It can be mounted in a room, entrance or corridor. It could also be made portable and used as a backdrop for an assembly looking at spring celebrations and festivals.

Preparation

Write large captions saying 'Spring celebrations' and 'Find out about special festivals and celebrations that happen in spring'. Make smaller labels saying 'Chinese New Year', 'Mothering Sunday', 'Holi - festival of colours', 'A special birthday', 'Pancake Day', May Day' and St David's Day'. Make other labels saying 'What happens at this special time?', 'What can you make from these ingredients?', 'Which is your favourite Hans Christian Anderson story?' and 'Can you find the country of Wales on the map?'. Decide where each festival and celebration will be arranged on the display. Place the labels to identify the festivals. Cut out the pictures.

Mount a selection of the posters and photographs onto card and add to the appropriate festival or celebration. Cut out and mount the calendar month of each festival and highlight the date. Place a label nearby giving the festival or celebration title. Photocopy pages 68, 76 and 78 with the poems and songs, 'Holi', 'Pancakes' and 'Maypole'. Mount these onto card and add to the display.

What to do

Set up the tables in front of the display area and cover with fabric. Back the display board with paper. Set up the display of children's paintings, collage and drawings. Enlist the children's help and ask them to suggest other captions. Invite the children to put out the objects on the tables.

Gather the children together and explain that the display shows special times and events that happen in the season of spring. Go through the different activities. Ask the children to find information and fictional books relating to spring festival and celebrations to add to the display. Encourage the children to help you decide where to put things.

Discussion

Gather the children round the display area. Talk about the special times that happen in spring. Encourage them to name some of these. Ask the children to describe what happens at these special times, for example making pancakes. Encourage them to describe what you do with the ingredients. Invite children to touch, feel, read and look at the objects, poems, songs and captions on the display.

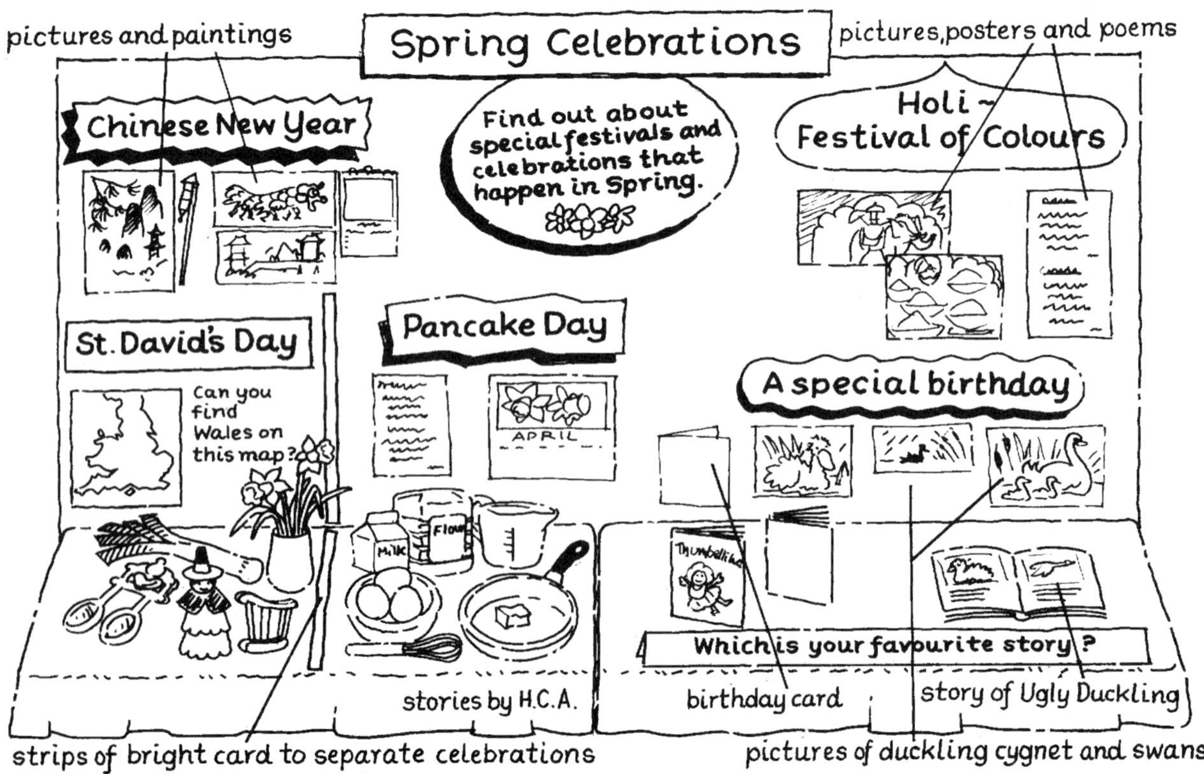

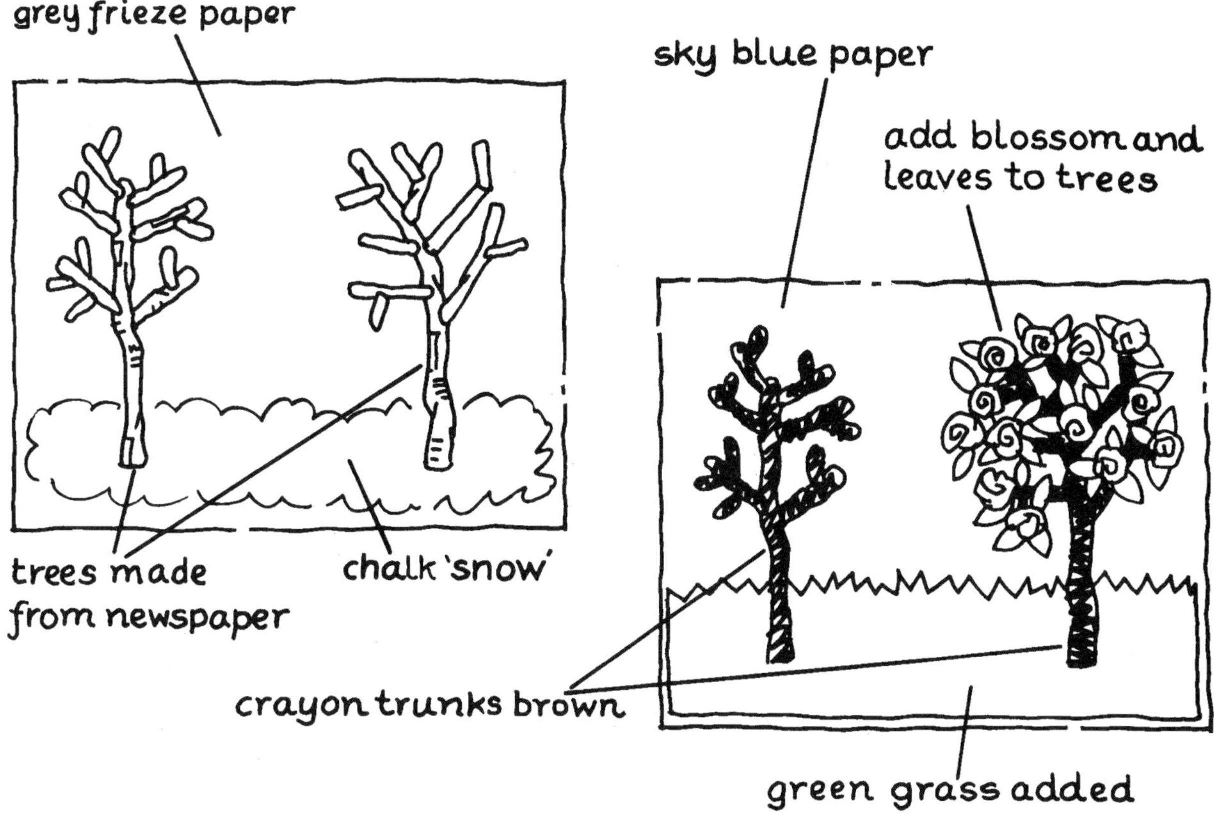

ALL CHANGE – WINTER TO SPRING

What you need

An area of wall space covered in grey frieze paper, newspaper, sheets of kitchen paper, adhesive, scissors, white chalk, pink and red tissue paper, strips of green fabric or paper, brown crayons and blue paint.

Preparation

Two craft sessions would be needed, with one taking place in January and the other following in March (this could be spread over a week each time).

What to do

Cover the wall with the grey frieze paper, preferably at a low level so that children can reach it. Using the kitchen paper as a base, assist the children, in pairs, to make collage trees out of torn newspaper. When the adhesive has dried, cut the trees out and mount them onto the grey frieze paper. Suggest that two children 'chalk' in the snow on the ground.

During the later sessions, show the children how to make 'blossom' by scrunching up pink or red tissue. Stick blossom on the trees on the right-hand side (spring), leaving the left-hand side trees bare (winter). The trunks can be coloured in brown. Children can stick green fabric or paper to make grass over the 'chalked-in' snow and paint some blue sky to complete the scene. Add the caption 'Change from winter to spring'.

Discussion

Talk firstly to the children about what the landscape looks like on a winter day, when it has snowed. Talk about the shapes of the trees and suggest they make some trees to place on the grey background.

Later, gather the children round the winter frieze. Ask how the world has changed (it will be a help if the children have been on a walk to look at spring blossoms). What has happened to some of the trees? How has the ground changed? What is different about the sky?

This display relates to the activities in Chapter 2 'Outdoor signs of spring'.

NEW BABIES

What you need

An area of wall space, a small table, large building bricks or boxes, light green or pale yellow frieze paper, a co-ordinating/contrasting drape. Coloured card, stapler, staples, Blu-Tack, scissors, a long piece of coloured tape or ribbon, thick black felt-tipped pens. Pictures and photographs of babies, kittens, puppies, lambs and young birds. A selection of first-size baby clothes and small toys, a tin of baby food, a small basket suitable for a kitten or puppy, a tin of puppy and kitten food, a bird's nest (ensure the nest has been abandoned and tell the children never to remove nests).

Preparation

Collect photographs and cut out baby pictures (such as babies, birds, lambs, kittens, puppies) from catalogues, magazines, greeting cards. Write or word-process a large caption saying 'Spring – a time for new babies'. Collect other baby items. Cut the card into smaller pieces.

What to do

Back the wall with the frieze paper. Place the table in position and arrange the bricks or boxes to provide different levels. Cover the table and boxes with a drape. Staple the caption onto the display board. Attach the photographs and pictures to the display board with staples or Blu-Tack. Place the objects on the table.

Gather the children around the display. Point out the pictures and photographs of the various babies. Invite the children to tell the name of the baby and what it will be when it grows up. Read the caption and explain that spring is a time for new babies for many creatures. Focus the children's attention on the objects on the table. Suggest that the items are needed by different babies. Encourage the children to identify the different items and say which baby would use them. Write the names of the items on the pieces of card and secure to the display.

Attach the coloured tape to the pictures and map it to the appropriate item, for example the baby bird pictures to the nest. Invite the children to suggest captions for the table items, for example 'human babies need special clothes', 'kittens can have special food'.

Discussion

Where do the birds build their nests? What food do new babies eat? Why does the farmer bring the ewe into the lambing sheds to have her babies? Explain that some babies are born in spring and some at other times. Which are spring babies? Which are 'anytime' babies?

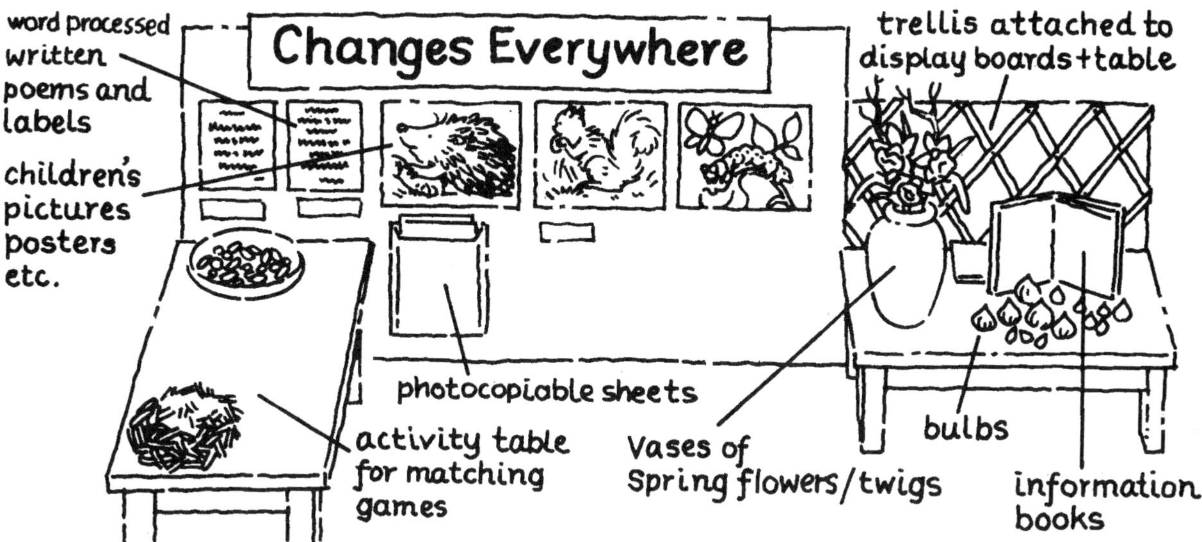

CHANGES EVERYWHERE

What you need

Portable screens or display boards, backing paper, two small tables, trellis, various boxes, scissors. Fabric to cover the table, staples, stapler, coloured thin and thick card, thick felt-tipped pens, crayons, paper, poster or powder paints, brushes. Pictures, posters, photographs, children's paintings and collages of creatures (hedgehogs, squirrels, frogs, chickens and hens, caterpillars and butterflies), a bird's nest (ensure the nest has been abandoned and tell the children never to remove nests), seeds, bulbs, daffodils, tulips. Calendar pictures of winter and spring scenes. Twigs, water, vases and spring flowers. Information and fictional books related to spring.

Preparation

Write large captions saying 'Changes everywhere' and 'Find out what happens in spring'. Make smaller labels saying 'What happens next?', 'Do you know who I am?' and 'Where did I come from?'. Cut out the pictures. Mount a selection of the posters and photographs onto card and add to the display. Mount the winter and spring scenes onto card. Make some into a matching game by cutting into sections. Photocopy the activity sheet 'What happens next' on page 90. Place these in a folder near the crayons. Photocopy page 70 with the poems 'It must be springtime', 'Seed needs', 'The gosling song' and 'Butterfly inside'. Mount these onto card and add to the display.

What to do

Set up the tables in front of the display area. Expand the trellis and fasten to the longest edge of one of the tables. Back the display board with paper. Place the boxes on and in front of the tables to give a three-dimensional effect and cover with the fabric. Set up the display of children's paintings, collage and drawings. Enlist the children's help and ask them to suggest captions.

Invite the children to put out the objects on the tables and box tops. Explain that the display shows changes that happen in spring. Talk about the different activities. Ask the children to find information and fictional books relating to spring to add to the display. Encourage them to help you decide where to put things.

Discussion

Gather the children round the display area. Talk about the changes that happen in spring. Encourage them to describe some of these such as frogspawn changing into tadpoles then frogs, eggs cracking and chickens coming out, seeds planted to grow into crops, bulbs which become spring flowers. Ask the children to describe what they think will happen to the twigs and flowers. Invite children to touch, feel, smell, read and look at the objects, poems, captions and activities on the display.

CHAPTER 8 ASSEMBLIES

This chapter suggests ideas for assemblies or group sharing times on the theme of 'Spring' and includes activities, prayers and songs.

CHANGE OF THE SEASONS

This assembly could be used as a general introduction to the topic. The focus is on the way people in olden days didn't understand the way in which the earth moves around the sun, making spring, summer, autumn and winter. People made up stories called 'myths' to explain what happened.

Help the children to design and make invitations for this event and involve them in the planning. Before the assembly, ask the children to suggest differences between winter and spring, summer and autumn. Write the children's suggestions on a large sheet of paper and ask them to paint pictures to illustrate the seasons. Read the children the 'Story of Persephone', on page 81, and invite them to play the roles of the characters. Before the assembly ensure that the children are well rehearsed. Learn the song 'New life' on page 80.

Introduction

Introduce the changing of the seasons by asking children to show their paintings. Encourage individual children to highlight differences between the seasons.

What to do

Explain how people made up stories to explain these changes and tell the story of Persephone. Introduce the children according to their roles.

Reflection

Lead the children to think how lucky we are to have the different seasons of autumn, winter, spring and summer. Encourage the children and visitors to think of things they like in the different seasons.

Prayer

Dear God, Thank you for the changes of the seasons. For daffodils and blossom, warmer days and lighter nights of spring. For summer days, fruits and flowers and bright blue skies. For the colours of autumn leaves, misty mornings and cooler days. For frosty winter mornings, bare trees and birds feeding in the garden, we thank you God. Amen.

Song

Sing 'Spring! Spring! Spring!' from the Resources section on page 73.

MOTHER'S DAY

This assembly focuses on the special day for mothers. It encourages children to think of things mothers do for us and the ways in which we can say 'thank you'.

Invite mothers, grandmothers or aunts to the assembly so they can share this special time with the children. Be sensitive to individual family circumstances.

Before the assembly, ask the children to paint or draw large pictures of their mothers doing things for them. Ask the children for simple captions. Scribe these onto card and attach them to the pictures. Mount these and display in a prominent position where the assembly is to be held, or ask children to show these during the assembly.

Give some children the responsibility to mime some of the things their mums do (cooking dinner, taking children to school, reading stories). These need to be well rehearsed. Involve the children in making Mother's Day cards, writing thank you letters and talking about things they might do on Mother's Day to help mums.

Introduction

Welcome the mothers, friends and other visitors. Explain that some mums, aunts and grandmas are not able to join in the assembly as they go to work or have other important things to do. It is a special time to remember mums, aunts or grandmas everywhere.

What to do

Ask the children to act out some of their mimes. Invite the audience to guess what is represented. Ask the children to read out their thank you letters, show their cards and pictures and explain what they might do on Mother's Day.

Reflection

Invite the children to sit quietly and think of things mums (aunts or grannies) do to help them. Encourage the children to think of things they can do to make their mums, aunts or grandmas happy.

Prayer

Dear God, Thank you for mothers, grandmas and aunts who look after us in different ways. Help us to remember how hard they work for us and remind us to say thank you and make them happy. Amen.

Song

Finish by singing 'Supermum' in ***Tinderbox*** (A & C Black).

CHANGES EVERYWHERE

This is an assembly that would fit in with many of the activities in Chapter 5. It focuses on the changes that happen in the spring. Learn the song 'Spring! Spring! Spring!' on page 73. Read the children the poem 'Wake up' from page 70. Write all except the last verse out on card and invite some children to say a verse. Teach all children the final verse. Choose some other children to dress up as hedgehogs, frogs, dormice and squirrels. Encourage them to practise waking up and moving as the creatures in the poem.

Before the assembly, make sure that all children are well rehearsed. Bring in an alarm clock and practise setting off the alarm just before the children say the last verse.

Introduction

Introduce the 'Changes everywhere' theme by asking children to guess what the assembly is going to be about from the clues you provide such as: 'The days get longer and the weather becomes warmer', 'It is the season that has March, April and May in it', 'People celebrate because winter is over'.

What to do

Start with the song 'Spring! Spring! Spring!'. Explain that spring is a special time when there are changes everywhere - in the garden, in the countryside, in our weather. Say that there are great celebrations all over the world to welcome these changes and the world wakes up after the long winter sleep. Invite the children to read out each verse of the poem 'Wake up'. Make sure they allow time for the children to carry out their mimes. Set off the alarm clock before the last verse, get all the children to stand up and say the final verse out loudly.

Reflection

Encourage children to think about the season of spring and all the wonderful things that happen. Help the children to realise that spring is an important time for plants, animals, creatures and people. Try and develop their awareness of the festivals and celebrations of other cultures, and events that took place many years ago.

Prayer

Dear God, Thank you for the spring. For the bright flowers, new leaves on the trees, the creatures waking up after their long winter sleep, and the new babies that are born. Help us to treasure this special time that sees changes everywhere. Amen.

Collective worship in schools

The assemblies outlined here are suitable for use with children in nurseries and playgroups, but would need to be adapted for use with pupils at registered schools. As a result of legislation enacted in 1944, 1988 and 1993, there are now specific points to be observed when develping a programme of Collective Acts of Worship in a school.

Further guidance will be available from your local SACRE – Standing Advisory Council for RE.

POEMS AND ACTION RHYMES

THE NEW SPRING HAT

My sister has a new Spring hat –
She wears it on her feet
And spends all day just bounding
First up, then down our street!
BOING!
She tried to wear it on her head
But then turned upside down –
And it gave her SUCH a headache
As she bounced around the town!
BOING!
She says she'll put her new hat
In a cupboard, out of sight –
And she'll listen to it bouncing
As she falls asleep each night...
BOING!

Trevor Harvey

APRIL FOOLS' DAY

On April Fools' Day Daddy said
He wished that he had stayed in bed,
For everywhere he went that day
Everyone had a joke to play
ON HIM!

Coral Rumble

WEATHERWISE

(Sing to the tune of 'If you're happy and you know it' – and don't forget to do the actions!)

Hold your hands in the air,
make a sun!
Curve your hands through the air,
make that sun!
Curve your hands through the air
make them draw a circle there.
Curve your hands through the air,
make a sun!

Wiggle fingers through the air,
make some rain!
Wiggle fingers through the air,
make that rain!
Wiggle fingers through the air,
make it rain everywhere.
Wiggle fingers through the air,
make it rain!

Huff and puff with your mouth,
make the wind!
Huff and puff with your mouth,
make that wind!
Huff and puff with your mouth,
north and east and west and south,
huff and puff with your mouth,
make the wind!

Judith Nicholls

I LIKE THE PARK

I like the park,
its tall oak trees,
its stately swans
and buzzing bees.

I like the lake
and waterfall.
I like to feel
the old brick wall.

Come to the park
with me today.
We'll walk and watch
and run and play.

Wes Magee

VISITING THE FARM

I'm visiting the farm again.
It's here, just down this little lane.
The gate is heavy,
Close it tight.
Rover's barking.
He won't bite.
See the cows, they're eating clover.
Here is the stile,
Let's climb over.
See the hens – clucking, scratching.
See the ducks – swimming, quacking.
Look in the barn – a calf so small.
There's a pig behind this wall!
MOLLY. TOM.
It's only me.
Have I got an egg for tea?

Margaret Willetts

HOLI

The bonfire roars.
Flames redden my face.
Our coconut's roasting
at the base.
Dad's telling the story
of Prahlad the good
while sparks fly up
from the crackling wood.

I love the bonfire's
fierce heat
and the special sweets
we get to eat.
But even better
than wood-scented smoke
are the stories of Krishna
and how he would joke.

We can do tricks
like the ones Krishna played,
throwing powder and being
splashed and sprayed.
Everyone screams and laughs
as they run.
Getting covered in colours
is always such fun!

Penny Kent

THE GOSLING SONG

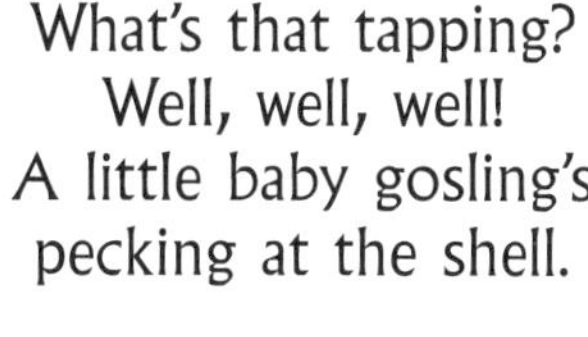

What's that tapping?
Well, well, well!
A little baby gosling's
pecking at the shell.

Here comes a beak,
and here comes a leg.
A little baby gosling's
hatching from an egg.

Out pops a head
and a fluffy yellow wing.
Then a cheepy little voice
begins to sing,

'Show me to the water.
Watch me, Mum.
See me swimming.
Here I come...'

SPLASH!

Tony Mitton

THE NEW NEST

Pick a twig here.
Pick a twig there.
Weave them together
With pieces of hair.

Leaves from the oak tree
And grass from the ground,
Weave them together
Around and around.

Line it with feathers
Or cotton or leaves.
A nest for my babies
Safe up in the trees.

Stevie Ann Wilde

BUTTERFLY INSIDE

Caterpillar long
(Stand up)
Caterpillar thin
(Arms straight by side)
Caterillar eat
(Eating actions)
Caterpillar spin
(Spinning action with hands)
Caterpillar hush
(Finger to lips)
Caterpillar hide
(Hands over face)
Caterpillar gone
(Open empty hands)
Butterfly inside!
(Join thumbs to 'fly' hands)

Coral Rumble

WAKE UP

Wake up prickly hedgehogs
with your beady little eyes.
Spring has come again
to give you a surprise.

Wake up little dormice,
the winter's gone away.
Uncurl yourselves and have a stretch,
the sun is out today.

Wake up sleepy squirrel,
and climb down from your drey,
and look for nuts you'd hidden
when the skies were cold and grey.

Wake up all you frogs,
at the bottom of the pool.
It's time to lay your spawn
in the water, deep and cool.

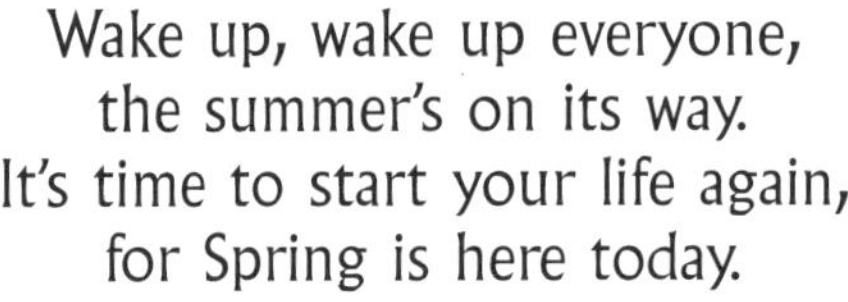

Wake up, wake up everyone,
the summer's on its way.
It's time to start your life again,
for Spring is here today.

Jan Pollard

IT MUST BE SPRINGTIME

Blossom dances
On the branches,
Lambs are leaping
Chicks are cheaping,
Children giggle
As tadpoles wriggle –
It must be Springtime!

Coral Rumble

MAD MARCH HARE

He runs so fast
with ears a-flopping.
There he goes,
and he's not stopping!

Wes Magee

TRUMPET OF SPRING

Blow your trumpet, daffodil,
And all the flowers will sing,
Then every garden in the land
Will celebrate the spring.

Coral Rumble

HERE COMES THE RAIN

Pitter, patter pitter, patter,
Hear the raindrops fall.
Splitter, splatter, splitter, splatter
Sharp against the wall.
Clitter, clatter, clitter, clatter
Here's a stormy shower.
Soft and slowly,
Swishy and squelchy,
Strong and stormy,
HERE COMES THE RAIN.

Janet Morris

WINTER TO SPRING

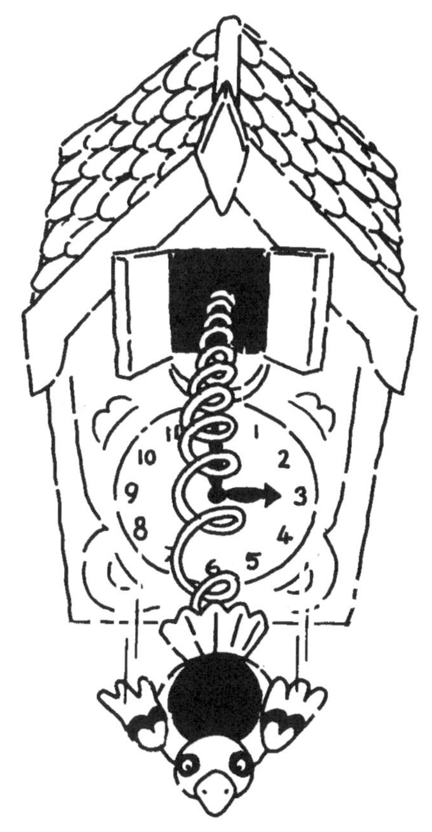

The cuckoo clock upon the wall
Tells the time
Tells the time
And every hour we hear it call:
'CUCKOO!'

A wooden door flies open wide
On the hour
On the hour
A clockwork cuckoo peeps outside:
'CUCKOO!'

Beside our house there stands a tree
Tall and strong
Tall and strong
And on one branch - what can it be?
'CUCKOO!'

The winter cold has gone away
Spring is here
Spring is here
A real live bird has come to say:
'CUCKOO!'

Trevor Harvey

VALENTINE'S DAY CARD

Sunshine's golden,
Skies are blue.
This card's to say
That ... I love you.

From,
Guess who?
Guess who?

Starshine's silver,
Moonbeams too.
This card's to say
My love ... is true.

From,
Guess who?
Guess who?

Wes Magee

SEED NEEDS

Here is a seed.
Leave it to sleep
under the soil
snuggled down deep.

Then when it wakes
down goes a root.
Up comes the tip
of a new green shoot.

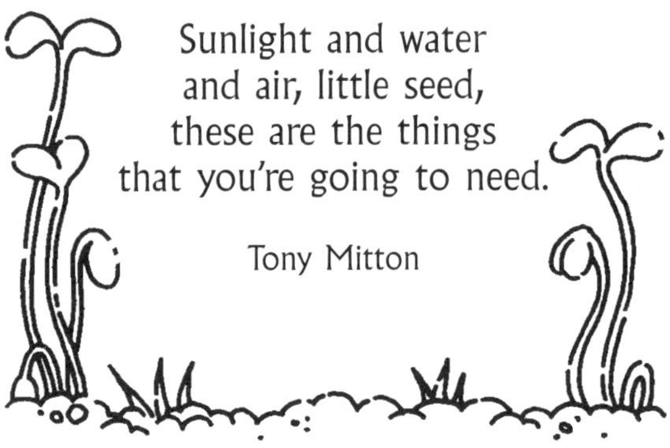

Sunlight and water
and air, little seed,
these are the things
that you're going to need.

Tony Mitton

SPRING CLEANING

In April or March
If the weather is fine
We spring clean our house
To make it all shine.
Brush, dust, polish and shake.
You'd never believe
The mess we all make!

Action: pretend to clean the Home Corner using the actions in the poem. Chant the poem as you work.

Susan Eames

SONGS

SPRING! SPRING! SPRING!

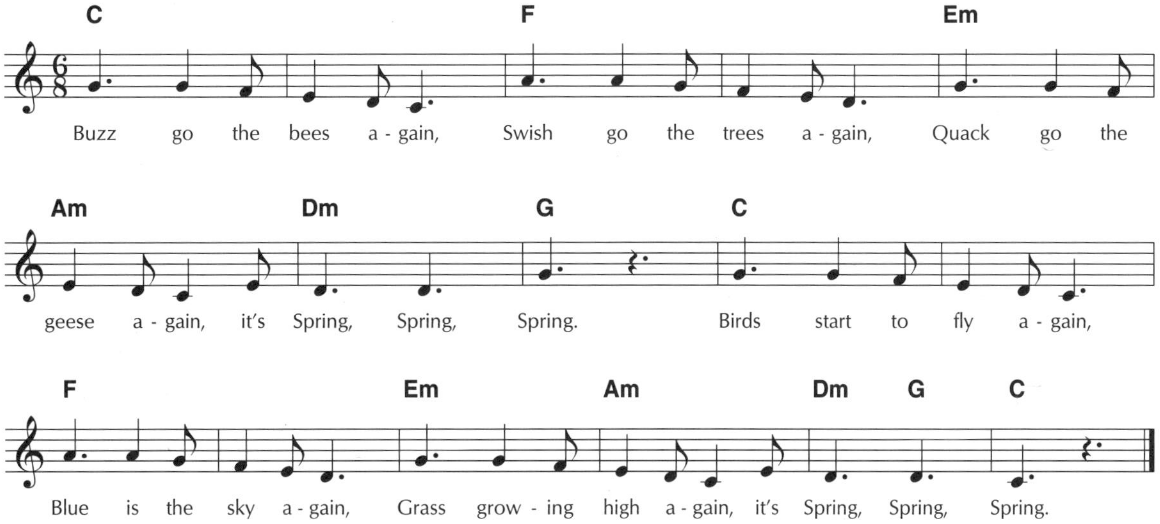

C F Em
Buzz go the bees a - gain, Swish go the trees a - gain, Quack go the

Am Dm G C
geese a - gain, it's Spring, Spring, Spring. Birds start to fly a - gain,

F Em Am Dm G C
Blue is the sky a - gain, Grass grow - ing high a - gain, it's Spring, Spring, Spring.

Clive Barnwell

SPRING BLOSSOM

A round

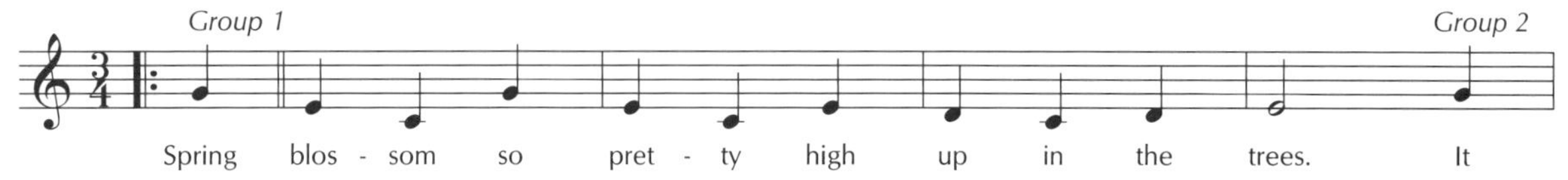

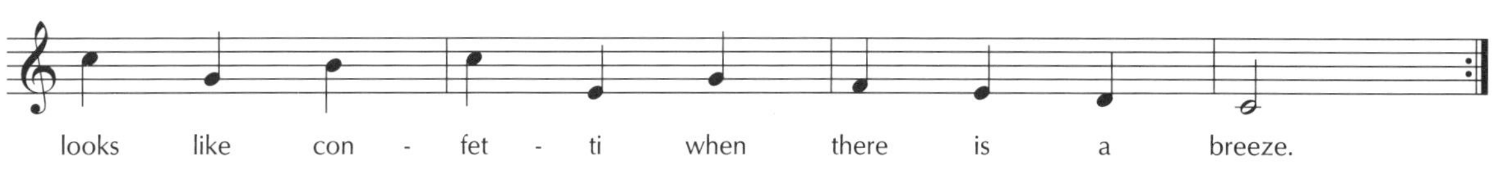

Johanne Levy

DAFFODIL

Slowly, stately

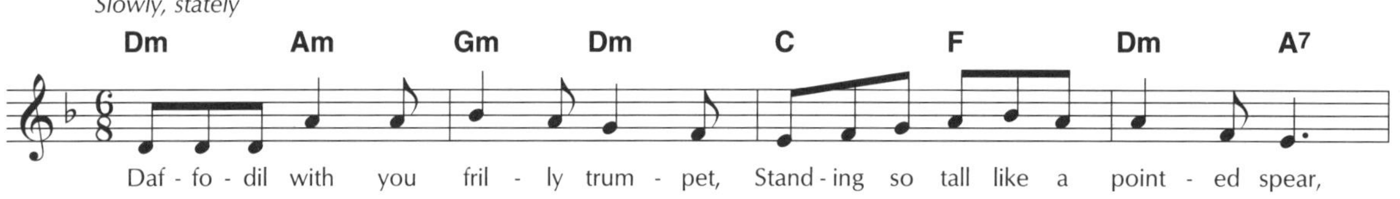

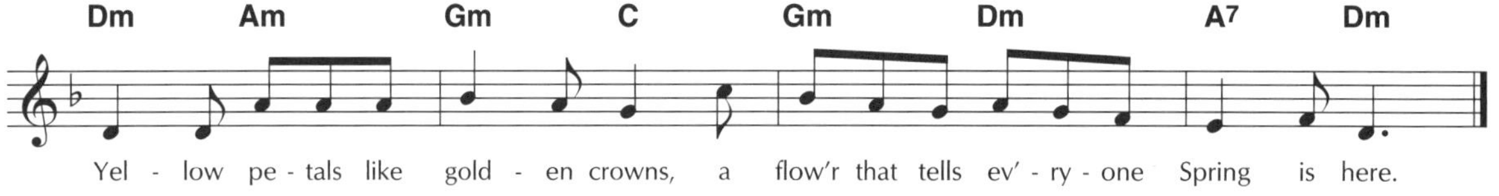

Sue Nicholls

I'M A FROG

2. *(Children wriggle about)*
Now I've hatched and I am wriggly (3 times)
I'm a little tadpole.

3. *(Children wave 'legs' about)*
Legs have grown now, 1, 2, 3, 4 (3 times)
I am nearly a frog.

4. *(Children wiggle a hand behind for a tail)*
Now my tail is getting shorter (3 times)
I'm a much bigger frog.

5. *(Children jump around a pond – imaginary or paper)*
Jumpy jump around the pond now (3 times)
I'm a fully-grown frog.

Susan Eames

MAYPOLE

Catherine Wheaton

IT'S BANK HOLIDAY MONDAY!

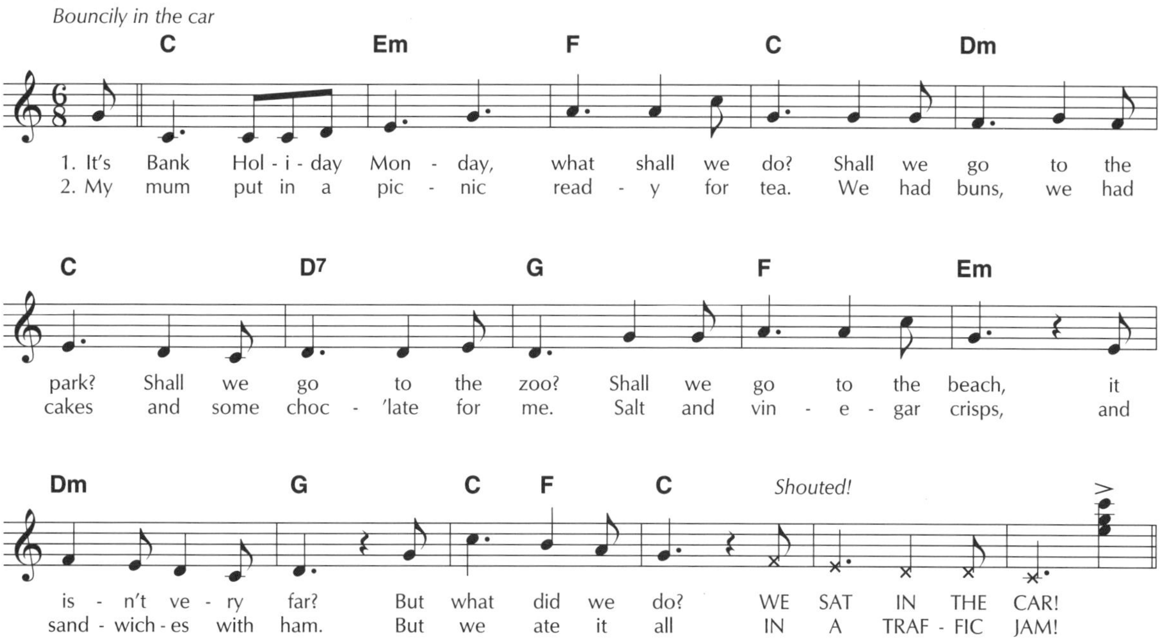

The children can pretend they are bouncing along in the car, holding the steering wheel.

Catherine Wheaton

PANCAKES

2. Take an egg,
Take some flour,
Stir them both with lots of power.
After beating, after heating,
We'll be eating pancakes soon.

3. Take some salt,
Take some milk,
Mix it 'til it's smooth as silk.
After beating, after heating,
We'll be eating pancakes soon.

4. Take a pan,
Take some fat,
Pour the batter round and flat.
After beating, after heating,
We'll be eating pancakes soon.

5. Take a chance,
When it's brown,
Toss and turn it upside down.
After beating, after heating,
We'll be eating pancakes soon.

Hazel Hobbs

SPRING CLEANING

Capo 1st fret

F/E — B♭/A — F/E

1. Wash the win - dows, Scrub the floors, Clean the cur - tains And the doors. Work all day,

C7/B7 — F/E — *Chorus* F/E — C7/B7

Wel - come Spring, Then we'll meet to dance and sing. Spring clean - ing, Spring clean - ing,

F/E — C/B — F/E — B♭/A — C7/B7 — F/E

Spring clean - ing time. Dus - ter, mop and broom Will clean up Win - ter grime.

2. Sweep the corners,
Tidy shelves,
Work away
Like busy elves.
Tidy up,
Here's the Spring,
Now we'll meet
To dance and sing.

Jean Gilbert

NEW LIFE

Based on The Selfish Giant
Add other verses by substituting for example – flowers, plants, crops, for 'trees'.

Ann Bryant

Hazel Hobbs

STORY OF PERSEPHONE

One sunny day Ceres (Mother Earth) and her daughter Persephone went walking in the woods. They looked at the beautiful flowers and green trees. Ceres returned home to plant some seeds, while Persephone walked further into the wood. As Persephone picked some flowers King Pluto of the Underworld rode by on his chariot. He saw the beautiful Persephone and decided to take her away to be his Queen. A water nymph watches as Persephone is taken back to the Underworld.

Ceres becomes worried about Persephone. She looks for her daughter in the woods until the Water Nymph tells her what has happened. Ceres is very sad. She decides that the world will be cold and dark with no flowers and no leaves on the trees until Persephone returns home. All the flowers wither and die. Trees shake off their leaves. Ceres makes the long journey to the Underworld. On the way she meets wild animals and creepy crawlies.

When she arrives at King Pluto's palace she finds Persephone is very happy and wishes to stay in the Underworld although she wants to be with her mother too. They decide that for half the year Persephone will live with King Pluto. For the other half of the year she will live in the world with Ceres. Ceres says that when her daughter lives in the Underworld the earth will be cold and dark. When she lives in the world the earth will be warm and light.

Retold by Anne Farr and Janet Morris

WAKE UP – IT'S SPRING!

All winter long, the ground beneath the trees in the wood had been hidden. The leaves which fell in the Autumn had formed a thick, squashy carpet everywhere, and now there was a layer of crisp, white snow on top. There was snow on the branches, too, making some of them dip heavily downwards. And underneath the many layers were the secret homes of woodland animals. Winter was a time for many of them to sleep.

Sheltered in the roots of a huge willow tree was the den of a mother fox and her new cub. The cub yawned and fidgeted while his mother licked him clean.

'May I go outside to play?' he asked.

'No, not yet, little one,' said his mother. 'You must wait for Spring.'

'What's that?' he asked.

'Spring is when the sun is warm again and the snow melts,' she told him.

The little cub wandered to the

entrance of the den, but the snow was cold and wet on his nose. He ran back to his mother and was soon asleep in her warm fur.

Far down in a burrow, in a warm nest of grass and soft fur, three baby rabbits climbed over their mother and tickled her long ears.

'May we go outside to play?' they asked.

'No, not yet, little ones. You must wait for Spring.' she said.

'What's that?' they asked.

'Spring is when the new leaves and shoots appear,' she said.

One little rabbit wandered away from the nest, but the walls of the burrows were cold and wet. He ran back and curled up with the others.

High in an old oak was the home of a mother squirrel and her family of four babies. They scrambled over their mother and played with her tail.

'May we go outside to play?' they asked.

'No, not yet, little ones. You must wait for Spring,' she said.

'What's that?' they asked.

'Spring is when the birds sing and flowers appear,' said their mother.

The little squirrels peeped out of the hole in the oak tree, but everywhere was cold, white and very quiet. They scuttled back to their mother and were soon asleep again.

The days passed. Gradually, the sun grew warmer and brighter and the snow and ice melted. Through the wood, a stream splashed noisily over rocks and stones.

Little fox cub woke up. What was that splashy noise? He looked out from the roots of the willow tree and saw the sparkling, racing water of the stream. The sun was warm on his face.

'Come quick, Mother!' he called. 'Spring is here!'

The sun shone into a clearing, where three baby rabbits crept out of their burrow and sniffed the air. It smelt good. All around, new shoots were growing through the carpet of leaves, and there were tiny green buds on the shrubs and trees.

'Come quick, Mother!' they cried. 'Spring is here!'

High in the branches of the oak tree, the squirrel babies chased and played. All around them, the birds were singing and collecting twigs and leaves for their new nests. Far below, they could see yellow primroses and wild daffodils. Suddenly, it seemed, the wood was full of sound and colour.

'Come quick, Mother!' they called. 'Spring is here!'

All day the baby animals tumbled and chased and skipped and played in the warm Spring sunshine, discovering new and exciting things about the wood around them.

'Little fox, are you enjoying the Spring?' asked mother fox. But there was no reply. Little fox was tired out from all his playing and was fast asleep in his den.

'Little rabbits, are you enjoying the Spring?' asked mother rabbit. But there was no reply. All her babies were tired from jumping and running and nibbling new grass. They were fast asleep in their burrow.

'Little squirrels, are you enjoying the Spring?' asked mother squirrel. But all the young squirrels were curled up into tight balls. All day they had played in the tree top in the sunshine and they were now very tired.

'Spring is a good time,' said their mother as she curled herself round them. 'But it's very tiring when you're new as well. Sleep tight, little ones. Tomorrow you can play again.'

Jackie Andrews

BOING! BOING! BOING!

'Spring's on the way,' said Mrs Gates from next door, looking over the garden fence to where Matthew's mum was washing her car.

'Yes,' agreed Matthew's mum. I love Springtime! It's my favourite time of the year.'

Matthew looked up from the mud pie he was mixing in a flower bed. He didn't usually bother listening to Mum and Mrs Gates – they talked about boring grown-up things – but this talk of 'springtime' was different. Matthew knew about springs.

Matthew loved asking lots of questions and finding out how things worked. For his third birthday, a few weeks ago, Gran had given him a Jack-in-a-box: a funny little clown that popped out of a box when you lifted the lid. Gran had shown him that between the clown and the bottom of the box was a thin coil of metal that wound round and round. It was called a spring.

The spring squashed down flat when the lid was shut and then sprang up when it was opened. Boing! it went, pushing Jack out of the box. Boing! Boing! Boing! Matthew thought springs were fun. And now it seemed that there was a special time of year called spring time. Interesting!

'Mum,' Matthew asked that night when she was tucking him into bed. 'Can you see the springs in spring time?'

'Oh, you see spring happening everywhere,' Mum answered.

'In our garden?'

'Oh yes,' said Mum. 'And in the countryside. There'll be little lambs, and rabbits and frogs. Springtime's a wonderful time of year.'

Matthew was thrilled. He lay in bed and imagined it – springs happening everywhere – boing, boing, boing! Little lambs and rabbits and frogs with springs underneath them, just like Jack the clown. Brilliant!

Where would they come from? How would they get into his garden? Maybe they'd bounce over the fence from Mrs Gates's: boing, boing, boing! across the grass? No. Matthew decided they'd probably spring out of the ground all over the place. Boing! There's a rabbit! Boing! And a frog! Boing! A lovely spring lamb! Oh, it was going to be wonderful.

Straight after breakfast, Matthew ran out into the garden. He stood for a long time staring at the lawn, so that after a while his mum came out to see what was wrong.

'Are you OK, Matthew?' she asked him.

'Yes,' he replied. 'I'm just watching for springtime.'

His mum was puzzled. 'But you can't watch for springtime,' she said. 'It's not like television.'

Matthew looked up. 'You said it happened everywhere,' he reminded her.

'Well, yes,' said his mum, 'but not all at once. I mean, Spring's quite a slow thing.'

'No, it's not,' said Matthew. 'Springs are quick. You press them down and they boing back again really fast. I've got to watch carefully or I might miss the rabbits and things.'

Matthew's mum smiled. 'Oh dear, Matthew. I think you're a bit mixed up.' She sat down beside him and explained that the word 'spring' has two different meanings. The spring in the Jack-in-a-box was one kind, and the spring of the year – when plants started to grow again and baby animals were born – was another.

Matthew was very disappointed. No baby animals were going to go boing! boing! boing! all over the lawn. 'Why do they call it Spring, then?' he cried angrily. 'It's silly!'

'No, it's not,' said his mum. 'Look.' She pointed to the bottom branches of a nearby tree. 'Can you see the tiny buds at the end of each twig?' Matthew looked. 'Well, there are little curled-up leaves in each one, just waiting to spring out and cover the trees. And down here on the ground –' she showed Matthew the small shoots of spring bulbs poking through the soil, '– these little shoots are going to uncurl and become daffodils and crocuses. That's why we call it Spring.'

Matthew thought it over. From what Mum had said, the world was going to spring into new life in the next few weeks, so he had been right in a way. And those little buds were interesting. He'd have to watch them carefully and try and figure out how they worked. In fact, it looked as if Spring might turn out to be quite an exciting time of year after all – even if it wasn't quite what he'd expected.

Sue Palmer

DAISY'S SPRING CLEAN

Yoohoo, Daisy! Are you ready to go shopping?' called Stella Rabbit, poking her head around the door of the big oak tree where her friend Daisy Squirrel lived. As usual, the house was in a mess. Clothes, bags and other things were scattered all over the floor and yesterday's supper dishes still hadn't been washed up.

'I'm in here,' Daisy called from the bedroom. 'I'm looking for my handbag. I won't be long.'

'Hurry up, or we'll miss the best bargains,' Stella said, walking into the bedroom. It was more of a mess than the lounge. Daisy was buried in the wardrobe, tossing things over her shoulder as she searched through it.

'My bag must be here somewhere,' came her muffled voice.

'What you need is a spring clean,' said Stella. 'It's no wonder you can't find anything with all this clutter around. You really must learn to tidy things away after you, Daisy.'

'Oh, I'm much too busy to keep tidying up,' Daisy told her, coming backwards out of the wardrobe. 'Anyway, I know where everything is – usually!'

'Well, you can't go shopping without your handbag,' Stella pointed out, 'and there's only one way to find it. We'll have to spring clean your house from top to bottom.'

'Oh no,' groaned Daisy. 'Then I'll never find anything at all.'

But Stella had put down her bag, taken off her coat, rolled up her sleeves and fetched the feather duster before Daisy could stop her.

'This won't take long if we do it together,' she said to Daisy. 'Come on!y. You tidy the bedroom and I'll tidy the lounge.' And off she went with the duster.

Daisy sighed and started tidying up. She put the clothes and shoes in her wardrobe, made her bed, picked up the books and magazines off the floor and put them in a cupboard. Then she vacuumed the carpet. She had to admit that it looked very good when she'd finished.

When Daisy went into the lounge she was amazed at how spick and span it was.

Everything was in its right place and the wooden table had been polished so much it sparkled. Stella was now in the kitchen, washing up.

'My house looks wonderful. Thank you, Stella,' smiled Daisy.

'You're welcome,' said Stella. 'Did you find your handbag?'

'Yes, it was under my bed.' Daisy smiled sheepishly.

'Good,' said Stella. 'Then let's go shopping.'

They both put on their coats and Daisy picked up her handbag. But now Stella couldn't find her bag. 'I remember I left it in your bedroom, Daisy,' she said. 'It shouldn't take long to find it now you've tidied up. I bet it's in your wardrobe.'

Stella marched into Daisy's bedroom and flung open the wardrobe door. Suddenly, everything fell out on top of her! Daisy had just thrown everything in there and shut the door! Poor Stella was now buried under a pile of clothes, shoes and other

things – and right on top of the pile was her handbag!

'There it is!' called Daisy, triumphantly, as she helped pull her friend out from under the heap. 'You were right, Stella. It's much better to tidy things away – then you know where they are!'

Karen King

THE SELFISH GIANT

Once there was a giant who lived in a house with a beautiful garden. It had green lawns, different sorts of trees and brightly coloured flowers. Birds and creatures lived happily in the garden. The giant liked nothing better than to walk in his garden and look at the changes through the seasons.

One day the giant received an invitation to visit his friend. He enjoyed his holiday so much he stayed for seven years! While he was away the children from nearby played in his garden. They ran over the green lawns, smelled the flowers and climbed the trees.

When the giant returned home he saw the children enjoying his garden and was very angry. 'Get out of my garden – and don't come back', shouted the giant in a booming voice. The children all ran away as fast as they could. The giant built a high wall around the garden and put up a huge sign that said 'KEEP OUT– TRESPASSERS WILL BE PROSECUTED'.

Spring came – bringing daffodils and tulips, and blossom on the trees. Birds sang their beautiful songs and began to build their nests. Creatures woke up after their long winter's sleep and filled their tummies with delicious food. Bees buzzed, butterflies fluttered and spotty ladybirds hurried along the plants. Everybody welcomed the spring after the long, dark days of winter.

But in the giant's garden it was still winter. There were no spring flowers, birds, insects or other creatures, only bare trees and brown soil. Frost, snow, hail, ice and the cold North Wind danced round the garden leaving signs of winter everywhere.

The giant kept looking out of his window. His garden still looked the same. 'I can't understand why Spring is so late,' said the giant. 'I was looking forward to warmer days and springtime in the garden.' Spring never arrived. Neither did Summer and Autumn. The giant kept looking out of his window. His garden still looked the same.

One morning the giant woke up suddenly. 'What's that?' he said to himself. He pulled the bed covers from over his shoulders and listened carefully. 'It's a bird singing,' said the giant with a broad smile on his face. 'IT'S A BIRD SINGING!' He hadn't heard a bird singing for such a long time. He jumped out of bed and rushed to the window. Outside the frost and snow had disappeared. There was no hail beating on the roof, no sound of the North Wind roaring. 'Has Spring come at last?' said the giant. He opened the window and leaned out. What a sight he saw!

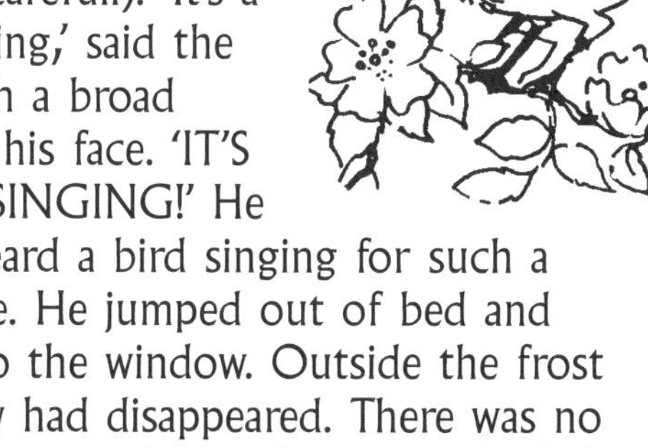

Children were creeping into his garden through a hole in the wall. They were playing on the grass and sitting in the trees. Flowers were peeping through the brown soil. Trees were covered with leaves and blossom was opening. Birds were singing as they flew around. The garden was so pleased to have the children back. Spring had come once more.

The giant looked around again. He was so happy. But what was that? In one far corner of the garden it was still winter. There was a tiny boy standing near a tree. It's branches were twinkling with silvery frost and snowflakes were fluttering down. The North Wind was howling and the branches were shaking as it raced through. The boy was so small he couldn't climb into the branches. He was walking round shivering and crying. The giant watched as the tree bent low as if it was trying to help the little

The giant looked at the small boy and his heart began to feel warmer. 'What a selfish old giant I've been,' he said. 'No wonder Spring didn't want to come to my garden.'

He went out and gently lifted the tiny boy into the tree. 'I'm sorry - I'll knock down the wall and you can all come and share my lovely garden. Come and play in here whenever you want,' he shouted.

And the selfish giant wasn't selfish any more.

Adapted by Anne Farr from The Selfish Giant
by Oscar Wilde

Odd one out

Look closely at the pictures and find the odd one out.

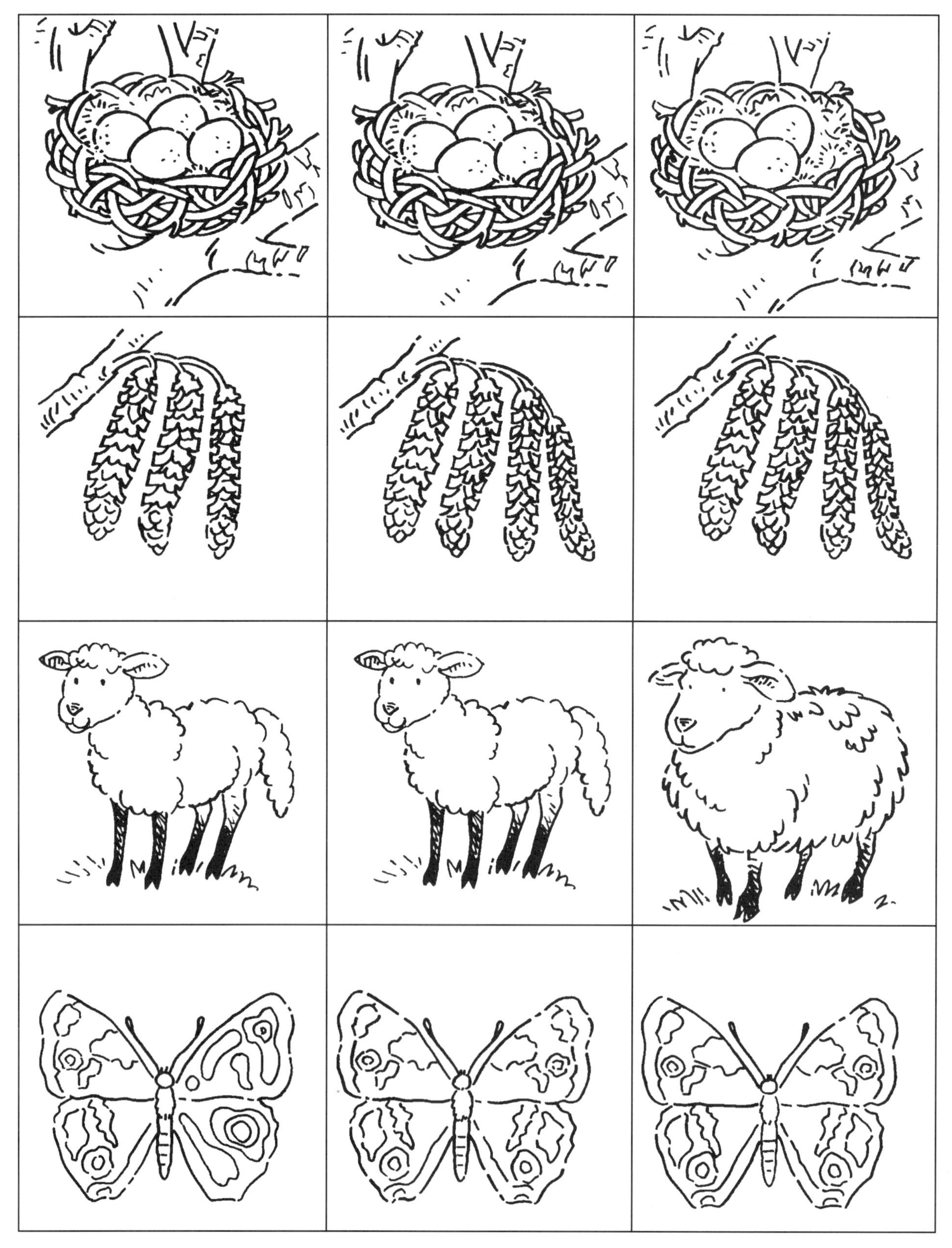

Signs of spring in our park

What to look for	Found	Spotted by … (enter child's name)
Snowdrops		
Crocuses		
Green shoots		
Catkins		
Heathers		
Something yellow		

THEMES
for early years

The park game

Throw the dice. Move your counter on the number of squares shown. If you land on a flower, go up the path. If you land on a stone, a patch of mud or a shower of rain, go down the slippery slope.

What happens next?

What do I use?

Find the things these people need for their work.
Join the items with a line to the right person.

Spot the ladybird game

Buzz off!

Draw the bee's journey.

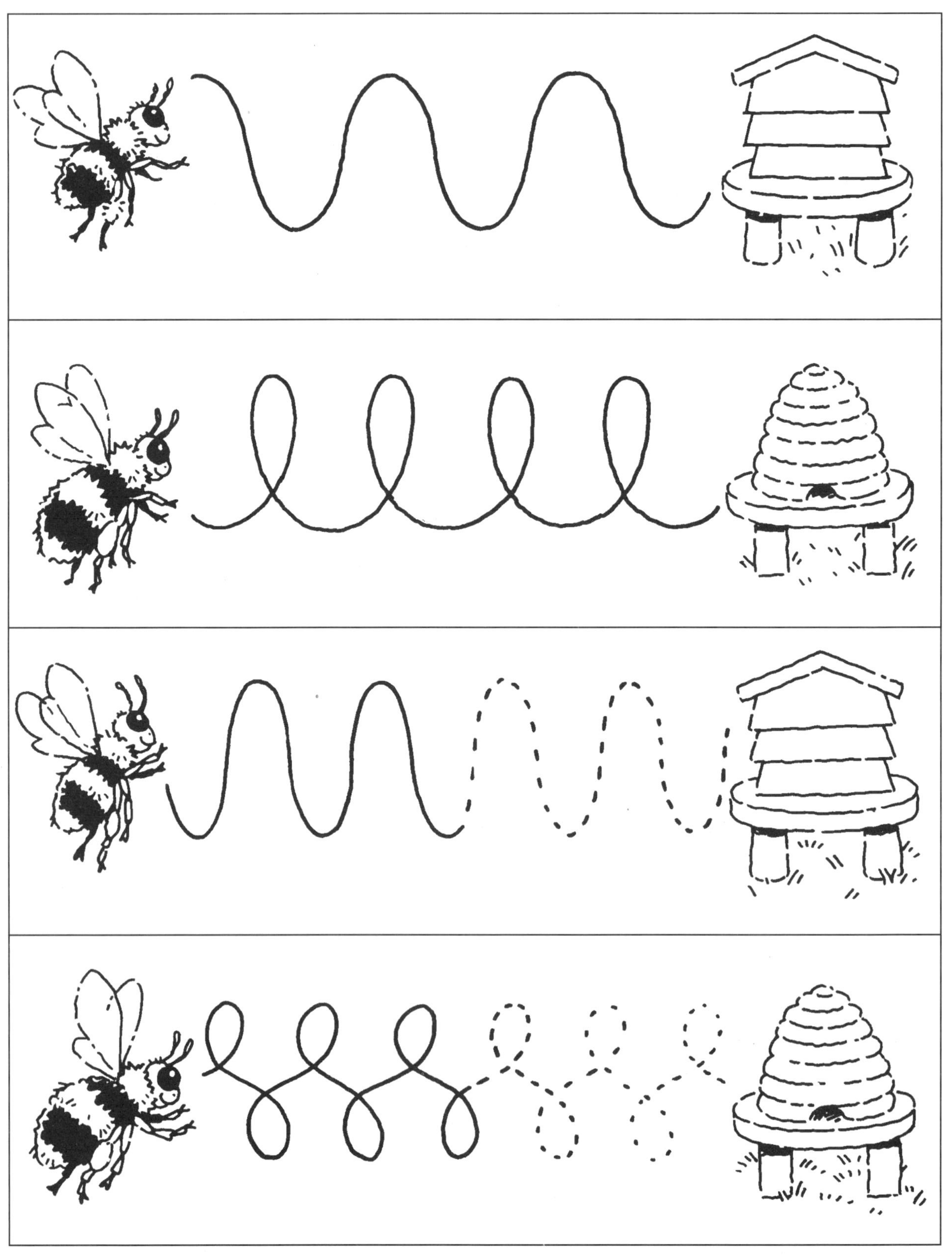

Building time

Cut out the pictures, stick them in the right order and colour them in.

RECOMMENDED RESOURCES

INFORMATION BOOKS

A Musical Calendar of Festivals Barbara Cass-Beggs (Ward Lock Educational)
Shrove Tuesday, Ash Wednesday and Mardi Gras Margaret Davidson (Welsh National Centre for Religious Education)
Festivals Meryl Doney, World Crafts series (Watts Books)
Spring Festivals Michael Rosen (Wayland)
Spring and Summer Festivals Themes for Early Years series Carole Court (Scholastic)
Spring Tinderbox Chris Deshpande and Julia Eccleshare (A & C Black)
We live in Australia Donna Bailey (Heinemann)

STORY BOOKS

When Willy Went to the Wedding Judith Kerr (Armada)
The North Wind and The Sun B Wildsmith (Oxford University Press)
The Baby Who Wouldn't Go To Bed Helen Cooper (Corgi)
Baby Goz: When I Grow Up Stephen Weatherill (Francis Lincoln)
Old Macdonald Had a Farm Prue Theobalds (Blackie)
The Spring Rabbit Joyce Dunbar (Anderson Press)
Jasper's Beanstalk Nick Butterworth and Mick Inkpen (Hodder Children's Books)

POETRY

'An Easter Chick' and 'An Egg for Easter' in *'The Book of a Thousand Poems'* J Murray Macbain (Harper Collins)
'Spring Song' in *'A Very First Poetry Book'* John Foster (Oxford University Press)
Let's Celebrate: Festival Poems (Collection) John Foster (Oxford University Press)
A Year Full of Poems Michael Harrison and Christopher Stuart-Clark (Oxford University Press)

MUSIC

A Musical Calendar of Festivals – Folk Songs of Feast Days and Holidays From Around the World Barbara Cass-Beggs (Ward Lock Educational)
Now is the Month of Maying Thomas Morley British Classics (Classic fM])
On Hearing the First Cuckoo in Spring Frederick Delius British Classics (Classic fM)
'Spring' from *The Four Seasons* Vivaldi Hall of Fame (Classic fM)
'Maypole dance' from *La Fille Mal Garde* Ferdinand Herold (Decca)
Spring Symphony Op.44 Benjamin Britten (Deutsche Grammophon)
'I went to the cabbages' from *Tinderbox* (A & C Black)
'The farmer comes to scatter the seeds' from *Someone's Singing Lord* (A & C Black)
'Could this be a sign?' from *Spring Tinderbox* (A & C Black)

ADDRESSES AND OTHER RESOURCES

'Spring Bird Table' and 'Woodpeckers in Spring' posters, 'Spring Birdsong' tape and the books *The Bird Table Book* by Tony Soper and *The Complete Garden Bird Book* by Mark Colley are all available from C J Wild Bird Foods Limited, The Rea, Upton Magna, Shrewsbury SY4 4UB.
The Birds in your Garden is a free publication available from RSPB, FREEPOST, The Lodge, Sandy, Bedfordshire SG19 2BR